JKAC

D0571694

The
Grumpy Golfer's
HANDBOOK

This book is dedicated to Hetty Hopkinson – cheaper than David Leadbetter and quicker to judgement.

Produced by Salamander Books, 2010

First published in the United Kingdom in 2010 by
Portico Books
10 Southcombe Street
London
W14 0RA

An imprint of Anova Books Company Ltd

ISBN 9781906032975

A CIP catalogue record for this book is available from the British Library.

10 9 8 7 6 5 4 3 2 1

Printed and bound by WS Bookwell, Finland

This book can be ordered direct from the publisher
at www.anovabooks.com

The Grumpy Golfer's HANDBOOK

Ivor Grump

PORTICO

CONTENTS

ADVICE FOR FOREIGN GOLFERS

SIMPLE MISTAKES

HOW TO MAKE ENEMIES ON THE COURSE

PANTHEON OF THE GRUMPS

GRUMPY GOLF MAGAZINE

INTRODUCTION

Somebody once said that golf and sex are the only two things you can enjoy without being any good at them. The big difference, of course, is that you know when you're really bad at golf because you have a scorecard to record your score on... and taking that kind of thing into the bedroom is never going to be much appreciated. Especially if you try and get her to sign it afterwards. (That might be one of those rare occasions when you think you scored an eight and your partner is keen to put down a four.)

Golf is a game that appeals to the obsessive compulsive side of men, their love of collecting statistics, and also their love of waving big clubs around. Sigmund Freud would have had a wonderful time analysing today's golf magazines and the kind of golf ball adverts that promise a penetrating trajectory and a "soft feel".

Because it's so important to them, men take golf very seriously, and that is why when it all goes wrong, as it inevitably will, they get particularly grumpy. Women are far too sensible to let golf affect them like that. As my daughter once said to me – "it's only golf, Daddy".

Even at an early age I knew I was destined to be a grumpy golfer. At 18, I was actually quite good at the game, club junior champion, a single-figure handicap with an assured touch around the green helped by a very trusty putter. Then one day my girlfriend Sally decided she wanted to accompany me on a round to see if this young "hotshot" was all he was cracked up to be. I wasn't sure this was a good idea. In fact, I was wary right from the start; even before she refused to carry my clubs down the first fairway (and at that age I could only afford eight). I knew that under scrutiny, the first poor shot or unlucky bounce would have me spitting the dummy, no matter how hard I tried to reign it in. My calm lasted till the fourth hole which was a long par-5 with a blind shot to the green at the bottom of a hill. I tried to make the green in two – way too ambitious – and sent a 4-wood into the valley below. When I heard the clatter of wood I knew I'd hit the dead elm trees to the right of the green and let out a sustained stream of expletives. Exit Sally towards the clubhouse: "You're such a child!" she said and sat under a tree for two hours reading *The Mayor of Casterbridge*, while I finished my round.

With age I've got worse not better. The teenage years made way for an angry young man, to an angry young man with children who didn't have the time and then a grumpy man who thinks he should be a lot better if only he had time to practise.

Through these pages you will share the joys, or otherwise (and mostly otherwise), of the many and varied grumpy golfing incidents from my career, plus those shared by my friends, relations and fellow club golfers.

The more perceptive reader might detect a scintilla of criticism of Americans and their attitudes to golf and I'd like to reassure anyone reading this book who hails from God's own country, that the sentiments expressed are only a bit of light banter and I'm only joshing with the stuff about Phil Mickelson and Boo Weekley. I'm sure in the case of the latter something *would* show up on an electroencephalogram, not just a message saying: "I'm not home right now."

If there is one particular chapter that I should direct you to, it's the one on Advice to Foreign Golfers. This, I feel, could make a real difference to golf tourism in the UK. In fact, I am going to suggest to the publisher that they try and syndicate it to a Japanese golfing magazine so that when their readers visit these shores, they are fully acquainted with our little foibles, our common courtesies – particularly the bit about interacting with slow female golfers. The Japanese are quite diligent in their observance of etiquette and I believe if they took some of these lessons on board this could mark a real watershed between our countries.

There is also a chapter where I've elected some golfers to the Pantheon of the Grumps. Naturally this is headed by our own marvellous Monty who can multi-grump from almost any part of a golf course. Whereas some just get a bit edgy on the tee or a bit cranky around the green, Colin can get grumpy from the moment he steps onto the practice ground. Which is good, as there are too many irritatingly controlled professionals in golf, which is a game sent by Beelzebub to test our resolve. As I think you'll gather from these pages, mine is normally tested by about the fifth stroke of the afternoon – somewhere between the first tee and the start of the fairway...

Ivor Grump

GOLFING WOES

The Nudge

The nudge is that excruciating beginner's mistake when you address the ball a little too closely and it bobbles forward off the tee. If you're playing with a friend then it's a given that you can replace it on the tee peg without incurring a stroke. Unless you've got money on the hole, at which point you might begin to see the monetary value of your friendship.

I like the golfers who, on the tee, assuredly whack the ball on the top with a downward motion, confident that as the clubhead is not going forward they won't incur a stroke penalty whatever happens to the ball.

Nudging in a competition is more costly, but by and large it's either a beginner's mistake or a facet of the Tourette's Syndrome golfer involuntarily twitching at the wrong ****ing moment, ****ing!

Away from the tee, nudging becomes less accidental and more deliberate, but we'll come on to that later.

The Hook

The hook is actually a lot better than a slice in that you can actually hit the ball a long way with a hook. I don't mind hitting long, loping hooks every once in a while, especially if they go as far as someone else's straight drive and don't end up in a badger's sett. I've always found that it's very easy to work out why you hook, because if you've got your feet in the right place, then you must be turning the clubface over before you hit the ball. This twisting of the clubface reaches its most profound expression in the snap hook. A snap hook happens so quickly that you don't have time to yell "Fore!" However, if there are ladies waiting to tee off, you do get to witness a scene of utter carnage on the Ladies' tee which is 40 yards further forward and to your left. With any luck a parked trolley or a strapping buttock will keep your ball in bounds and maybe even bounce it back on the fairway.

Of course, if you want to wind a deliberate hook around the corner of a dog-leg and set yourself up in the appropriate closed stance, then Grump's Third Law of Golf will dictate that you hit the sweetest, straightest shot you will make all afternoon...

Grump's Third Law Of Golf

Whenever you take an adapted stance to 'fashion a shot', i.e. bend the ball right to left, scoot it low, or try to get a lot of height, then the ball will always go unerringly straight and on a normal trajectory.

The Slice

Slicing a ball can be a nasty habit to get into. On the archetypal links course it could put you in the sea nine times unless you were meteorologically savvy enough to go out only when there was a strengthening onshore breeze.

Natural slicers love the wide open prairies of new golf courses and the lack of confines that parkland fairways afford. Not for them the narrow strictures of the 12th hole at Wentworth or the 18th at Augusta (though doubtless 'having a bit of a slice' isn't going to be the biggest barrier to playing either of those two courses).

I always put the slice down to one of two things: it's either a laziness in the stroke, where the golfing genie that sits on my shoulder just can't be arsed to straighten the clubface in time. Or it's a crisis of confidence in the downswing. 'I know I mustn't slice on this hole, there's a lake over there, it's deep, there are piranha, that's your lucky golf ball, your round's going really well, don't b****r it up with a slice now, you cretin'.

I mean, that's an open invitation to slice. It's like when I meet an attractive young woman showing a lot of cleavage. I know that if my eyes focus anywhere below her forehead then they're going to be dragged downward like a divining rod that's just discovered the Queen Elizabeth reservoir beneath it. I keep my eyes up for as long as I can, but a woman's cleavage has its own gravitational pull. And the second your eyes get wrenched downwards she looks at you pityingly as though you were the Uncle Ernie character from *Tommy* the musical (the part that Keith Moon played who liked to 'fiddle about' and wore a raincoat).

So in these intimidating circumstances I am likely to hit a great fat banana split of a slice. And there's nothing I can do about it. Because if I alter my stance and deliberately aim to the left, then Grump's Third Law kicks in which will ensure that I hit a perfectly straight shot out of bounds to the left.

The Shank

The shank is a nasty reminder that golf can hurt sometimes. Like the complete duff, it usually happens when you try and belt the logo off the ball. You swing harder and wider than you normally would and the heel of the shaft makes a clanging connection with the ball sending it scuttering along the fairway while your club vibrates with all the sustain of a vintage Gibson Les Paul.

This vibration is gleefully transferred up the shaft to your hands in a kind of Tom and Jerry stylee. The seismic effect of a shank can plague you for the rest of the hole. Longer in cold weather. It's not as bad as hitting a tree with a golf club, but at least you know there's a possibility of the tree coming.

The Air Shot

An air shot from the tee is even more embarrassing than a nudge or a duff. Thankfully these days there is an almost believable excuse at hand. With the rise of Big Bertha drivers it's quite common to see golfers swinging a small (titanium) bungalow on the end of a graphite shaft. To whack the ball successfully and not excavate a small trench in the turf, they need lofty tees the size of six inch nails. When I first saw them on sale in a golf shop, it was one of those 'I don't quite believe it' kind of moments – like watching Alistair Campbell getting "tired and emotional" on television. Balancing a ball on top of one of these tees must require some kind of training at the Chinese State Circus.

Anyway, swing and miss and you can come out with the quite plausible, "Doh, I thought I was swinging with the big driver…" Unless of course you *were* swinging with the big driver.

Air shots in the rough, especially deep rough, have little or no stigma attached. There's hardly an Open

Championship goes by without an air shot from somebody who thought they might find their way out of the middle of a clump of heather. Usually John Daly.

Air shots on the fairway are harder to explain away. Air shots on the putting green? You might as well get your coat and transfer your golfing prowess to a sporting venue that deserves your level of skill, i.e. putting through a windmill into a clown's mouth.

The Duff

You can hit duff shots, have a duff round, but a good old-fashioned duff is a hefty club/ground interface where mud flies. I'm defining a duff as when you aim to hit the ball 300 yards and end up hitting a divot 30 yards and the ball five. Duffs are particularly frustrating for a golfer who normally makes a good score and can break 90. For those that are riddled with the duff, then it's not frustrating, it's their *modus operandi*, the way they get round 18 holes.

In fact 'riddled with the duff' sounds like it ought to take its place somewhere in Samuel Pepys' diary:

May 7th, Lord's Day
Up betimes and met my Lords Sandwich and Sir William Coventry and very merry, too. They enquired if I would take a game of golfe with them, but I confessed I was riddled with the duffe.

Duffs happen when golfers sense a moment of glory, the chance to hit a majestic shot that belies their handicap and gives a sense of true golfing genius. And then they go and blat the clubhead into the turf.

The duff happens because golfers have a rush of blood to the head. They get excited and lift their head in anticipation of seeing the ball hurtle arrow-straight up the fairway or shoot down the throat of the flagstick.

*See also The Fluff/Duff Recovery (Page 74)

The Thin

This is the yang of the duff's yin. Whereas the duff is too much ground and very little ball, the 'thin' is too much ball and no ground at all. Thinning is most prevalent around the green where a delicate little chip is required.

Instead of popping the ball up onto the putting surface, the thinner hits the ball midships transforming his pitching wedge into a 2-iron. The result is that a 15-yard lob is transformed into a 50-yard small bazooka round, scattering your unsuspecting playing partners who are preparing to putt out on the green. A golfing friend thought he would have a major lawsuit on his hands while playing up to the 18th green of an unnamed golf course (but it's in Kent, not far from Ashford). The clubhouse bar overlooked the 18th green and hence most times of the day there was an audience to impress. It had been very wet, so he thought he could fly it straight at the pin with a sand wedge. He took a full swing of the club, looked up as he swung through, hit the ball midships and sent it at head height straight into the clubhouse window. (Sadly all the golf balls he'd ever lost didn't flash before his eyes as this happened). It was to his great relief that the club's owners had foreseen the likelihood of such an occurrence and he discovered that it was a plate glass window.

Yips And Yippers

Forgive my lack of empathy but I have no time for yippers. Anyone who can get spooked out by a short putt has lost their sense of proportion. Yippers are all mummy's boys. "Are you gonna miss the nasty ickle putt then." Get a grip of yourself man!

For most of us, the titanic struggle is to get to the green in the first place. When you're on the green you're home; what's the worst that's going to happen there? On the odd occasion you might four-putt (and to be fair, I have putted into a bunker before), occasionally you'll three-putt, a lot of the time you'll two-putt and every once in a while you'll only need one putt. What's so pant-wettingly scary about that?

The blue blanket for yippers is the long broom handle putter. Having one of those is like wearing incontinence pants over your golfing trousers. It's a very public admission of psychological frailty.

N.B. Bernhard, no-one ever remembers that little putt you missed to lose us the Ryder Cup and it's rarely if ever talked about.

The Toe Shot

No, not an old reference to that photo of Fergie by the swimming pool in the South of France with her financial advisor, this is a different stroke. I've got a lot of affection for the toe shot. And by this I mean a tee shot, or fairway wood, where you swing inside the ball and connect with the toe of the club, wafting it out to the right before it bends gracefully (if a little limply) back in. It's like a football free-kick bent around a wall and I suppose the spin on the ball must be similar.

If I were to choose any of the golfing faults then a toe shot would be the mildest.

My order of *least* preference would be:

Nudge

Air shot

Duff

Shank

Slice

Hook

Yip

Toe shot

On a good day my brother can produce most of these on a par-5 hole and on the subsequent hole throw in his speciality – the Unsuspected VTOL shot.

The Unsuspected VTOL Shot

When I saw it for the first time it was a wonder to behold. My brother strode up to the sixth tee of the Worcestershire Golf Club with his not particularly trusty 3-wood. His swing was smooth, he made a cracking connection and we both stared down the fairway trying to see if he'd missed the copse on the right of the fairway at 200 yards. But neither of us could work out where it had gone.

"Did you see it…?" he asked.

"Er... not exactly." I replied.

Then, after what seemed like an age it plopped down onto the fairway 15 yards in front of us. A quick discussion of golf ball physics divined that it had come off the very top of the club and done a Hawker Harrier Vertical Take Off and Landing (VTOL), shot 150 yards into the air and then come down again.

It's a shot he's repeated in various forms over the years. While chefs have their signature dishes, he's got his signature crap shot.

He has to be careful when he goes to covered driving ranges that the cover over his particular booth isn't too generous. He's never been to a two-tier range but I guess that might be exciting, too. One time, during a winter Stableford, he decided to take a wood on a tricky par-3. Normally he'd take a 5-iron on that hole, but he was hitting into the teeth of a gale and so opted for the extra punch. He produced his signature shot, skied the ball and managed to land the ball 20 yards behind him at the back of the tee.

I'd love to say that he hit a brilliant recovery shot to within three feet of the pin and holed it for the most amazing par, but sadly he hit the tee block on the way back.

PR For Crap Shots

In this PR-obsessed PC world, (and we're not talking about the computer store) where there are no longer "problems" only "challenges", where failure has to be dressed up as achievement only on a different level, the poor golf shot can easily be made extinct. If you apply the same levels of spin we get on political items, then run it through a PR filter, the crap shot comes out scrubbed up, clean and looking very pleased with itself.

It's no longer a slice, it's a "generous fade". That wasn't a hook it was an "energetic draw". Your ball didn't just trickle into a bunker through under-clubbing, you opted for "a sandy lay-up". It's not a duff, it's a "reduced-face impact"; it's not a shank, it's a cheeky little "mole worrier"; it's not a yip, it's merely an early round "green tester". Or if it happens later in the round, it's an "atypical aberrant hyper-extended motor neurone functionality error."

And if you think that's a load of b*******t, try being a political journalist.

IN THE CLUBHOUSE

Dress Code

Though dress code applies just as much on the golf course as in the clubhouse, it's in and around the clubhouse that the wrong sort of schmutter is likely to be picked up. The underlyingly laughable thing about 'proper golf attire' is that the dress code rules were thought up by people who think Dunn & Co still exist and that we still possess India.

The irony being that most meths-swigging city centre winos would pass the dress code for your standard golf course (with an endearing crumpledness of course) while West Coast senior executives for multi-billion grossing software companies would not. The difference being that the software moguls will have paid four figure sums for their denim on Fifth Avenue and Rodeo Drive, whilst the winos will have got their tweeds out of the Humana clothes recycling bin.

No Actual Code For Dresses

The standard dress code for a golf club runs along the lines of:

"Collared golf shirts must be worn at all times on the golf course and must be tucked into the waist band."

A golf shirt being one where the designer has carefully chosen a blend of patterns at least 15 years out of date and employed nothing but the finest synthetic materials known to man.

"Shorts may be worn provided they are tailored in style and of Bermuda style length."

There is seemingly no restrictions on you cutting out the arse cheeks to reveal that you're going (Penfold) commando.

"Socks must be worn and be above the ankle for men."

And preferably above the knee also. It's an underrated look.

"Golf caps may be worn provided the peak is pointing forward."

As if anybody who bought anything so prosaic as a 'golf cap' from an official 'golf cap shop' would ever have 'homies', a 'hood' or turn it round backwards to look cool. There's a significant absence of bling on display in most clubhouses and you very rarely come across a couple of chaps on the 8th tee discussing their ICE systems or discussing how fond their bitches are of their pimped up new Lexus.

"Ladies may wear sleeveless shirts with a collar."
Ladies may wear lycra catsuits, a bikini or a burka, but sleeveless collared shirts are the Pringle tartan jumper of female golf.

"The following are prohibited from the course: denim, short shorts, tennis length skirts, tee-shirts, tank tops and sweatshirts."
For the above read: "crimplene, beige, tartan trousers and anything with a pom-pom."

Seriously, are they really suggesting that if Natalie Gulbis turned up at your golf club wearing one of her *waffer theen* golf skirts and asked if she could play a round that the club secretary would actually stop her because of what she was wearing? There'd be a riot.

The Pringle-Style Tartan Jumper

As far as this author is concerned, random death squads should be allowed to roam loose on Britain's golf courses to take out anyone they find wearing a Pringle-style tartan jumper. Unless someone was wearing it ironically, but that's a bit of a judgement call.

It's not so much a crime of fashion, it's more a

crime against humanity. It would be fair enough if this first degree visual offence were going to be inflicted exclusively on other golfers but occasionally civilians get to witness them and that is just not acceptable in this day and age.

Men who wear tartan-style jumpers to play golf have the creative imagination of a trowel. "It's what golfers wear so I should wear it," is their logic. Along with Farrah polyester slacks. If I had my way I'd like every golfer to dress like Ian Poulter or Payne Stewart (god rest his soul) and even at times John Daly.

Old School Stewards

One of the outstanding songs in the long-running West End musical, *Les Miserables* is about the customs and habits of Thenadier, the inn-keeper. If the name doesn't ring a bell then how about the song "Master of the House"? Alain Boubil's lyrics, translated by Herbert Kretzmer, describe Thenadier as, "watering the wine, making up the weight, picking up their nick-nacks when they can't see straight."

If Thenadier had lived in the twentieth century then he most certainly would have ended up as a golf club steward.

Golf Club Bars

They've come on a lot since the 1970s and 1980s, but golf club bars used to be like a rock star's home pub: a few optics, a limited number of beers on draught and nobody about most of the time. In the bad old days before the democratization of golf, when it was much tougher to join a club, you would get a snobby crowd in golf club bars. It was like a cross-section of a normal pub, but someone had taken out all the normal people, the women and children and replaced them with blokes who talked too loud. Thankfully, with the oversupply of golf courses and the various financial woes, they're no longer stuffed full of freemasons, chartered accountants and retired bank managers; it's a younger, more proletarian game and the better for it. Nowadays there are spikes bars, so if you don't want to drag yourself to the changing room and get changed into your Leslie Phillips/Terry Thomas blazer and cravat, you can walk into the spikes bar and happily start spiking people's drinks. And even in spikes bars the eternal rule applies: the louder the punter the worse he is at the game.

Parking Spaces

When you get to a golf club there are special reserved parking spaces for the Captain, Secretary, Ladies Captain etc which means that the best three places to park are not used for most of the week. This is highly inefficient and just adds to the congestion for the rest of us. It's a symbol of rank and as the people's golfer you'd expect me to storm the barricades of privilege and tear down the walls of exclusivity. Far from it. I don't think the signs go nearly far enough. Let's get prescriptive. They should have parking spaces for the Professional, the Assistant Professional, the Head Greenkeeper, the Handicap Committee, Reg the bloke who always sits on a stool by the bar hoping to talk to people… Let's fill the whole car park up with signs, then there are far more opportunities to p*** someone off by parking in their space.

ETIQUETTE

Good Manners Cost Nothing

It's only when you introduce someone new to golf that you realise how much etiquette the sport has wrapped itself up in. Taking a complete novice onto a golf course can be a wearying experience. You have to constantly remind them where to stand, where to walk, when to stop walking, when to stop talking, when to take the flag out and why they shouldn't jab the end of the flagstick into the green.

A lot of the dos and don'ts of golf are simply down to good manners; DO compliment your playing partner on any good shot he or she should make, DON'T break wind loudly when they are teeing off. You wouldn't do it in the bar afterwards, so why do it on the tricky 6th hole par-3 over water. It's common courtesy. The following chapter could be excerpted and sent to any new member applying to a golf club.

Quiet On The First Tee

It's only fair that you give your opponents (if it's a competition) or your playing partners (if it's a casual round) every chance to make a decent stroke. While they are attempting a practice swing it's okay to chat and banter. However, once they address the ball for their shot, one should keep quiet. This is most important on the tee when you are in close proximity to your fellow players, but it should also carry through to shots on the fairway and on the green, where most club golfers meet up again. It's not just the talking that has to stop, one should also refrain from coughing, spotting woodpeckers, yodelling, belching, breaking wind or receiving a mobile phone call.

Mobile Phones - Is It Good To Talk?

There is a tremendous temptation to take your mobile onto the golf course. For many company executives it is their 'blue blanket' and to go for three hours without having the reassurance that their business hasn't gone under is too much to bear. Many clubs ban them. And they're right to. I read a plea in one of the golfing magazines by the BBC's excellent golf correspondent Ian Carter that they should be tolerated on the golf course provided they are switched to silent.

No.

It's poking a toe over the edge of a slippery slope. The golf course is a sanctuary, a refuge, an escape from the modern world. And to treat it otherwise is to treat it with disdain. How long is it before we have internet access points between the 9th green and 10th tee? How long it is before someone orders a take-away pizza on their mobile and gets it delivered to the 14th green?

When mobile phones are banned from courses, golfers have a legitimate excuse not to talk to the wife or girlfriend or employer about their whereabouts. They have a glorious few hours to concentrate their attention on their golf and the companionship of playing it. Attending to texts or phone calls dilutes the experience.

Golf courses should be the equivalent of a space shuttle re-entering the earth's atmosphere – absolute radio silence. There is nothing more irritating than listening to another golfer yabbering away into his mobile phone on the fairway opposite you and I'm all for allowing golfers to have a 15th club, providing that 15th club is a sniper rifle.

The Myth Of Divots

When you carve a great lump out of the fairway with a 5-iron you will be expected to chase after the divot and replace it. This is part of one of the great myths of golf. That replacing divots is any use at all. Divot regrowing is about as successful as male hair transplants. A patchy threadbare non-event. Most of them are made in summer (that's the divots, not the hair transplants) and the grass, disconnected from its root system, dries out and dies. Many times the divot turns into an explosion of grass and earth and cannot be put back together again.

Replacing a divot is only useful in preventing another ball from rolling into the same scrape hole and another golfer excavating it out with a 5-iron and starting the onset of serious soil erosion. It is also one of the 'done things' on a golf course so everyone has to do it. Not doing it means you are a bounder.

Trolleys

Some golfers have trolleys, a few geriatric ones – for whom the zimmer beckons – have motorised trolleys and fat lazy b******s have golf buggies. There is no need to have a golf buggy in the UK unless you are an American tourist for whom the idea of putting one foot in front of the other to get somewhere is an alien concept. Golf buggies are fine in the Caribbean or in Florida where the heat and humidity really takes it out of you, but in the UK they are not necessary. They're more likely to be taken joyriding down the M4 by a drunken Welsh rugby star than serve any useful purpose.

Trolleys on the golf course have their own routes and paths marked out that thread their way around tees and greens and it is etiquette that these are followed. The only difficult part is the transition from being a golf bag toter to a trolley wielder on a familiar course. It's difficult to shake off that feeling that you can wander anywhere you like – the way you did with your bag for all those years – and you have to come to terms with the fact that your freedom has been curtailed and you have to follow the path now. In many ways it's like parenthood. But not so many disposable nappies.

See also Sundry Irritations (page 116)

The Honour

The person who has 'the honour' is the golfer who believes he scored the lowest on the previous hole. That person has the honour of clubbing their ball into the scenery first on the next hole. From that point on it's the golfer who is furthest from the hole who should play first – unless of course they've driven onto another fairway and are waiting for a gap in the traffic.

Losing It

No matter how much you think your playing partner is a turd, it's only polite to go and help him look for his ball when it heads for the long grass. You don't have to look – obviously – you only have to appear to be looking. In the trade it's known as the 'I'm looking but I'm not really looking' foot swish. You poke the grass with one foot and then the other, like some half-hearted country dancing at the W.I. At the same time you mutter gratuitously false sentiments such as "I'm sure it's some-where round here. It should be really easy to find."

The only contentious lost balls are when someone insists on continuing to look for a ball when it's well over the five minutes and someone is waiting to play through. Also, when the ball heads into uncharted territory, into gorse, heather or brambles where there is little hope of retrieving it even if you can see it. These are the flashpoints that tell you whether you are going to avoid playing golf with this person ever again. Or even for another hole.

You Want It, Or Don't You?

I have never quite worked out the etiquette of what happens if you find another golf ball, while looking for your playing partner's ball. As a teenager in the 1970s they were such a high-budget item that if your mate lost one, you would immediately give him the one you found if his turned out to be lost. You could only honourably keep the second ball that turned up.

Fast forward to the 21st century when golf balls are relatively cheap and our earning power significantly higher than at age 14. Do you offer the found ball or is that an unwanted act of charity? On a company golf day I proffered a ball to someone who'd already put two into the woods by about the 7th hole and he looked at me as though I'd just mugged a tramp for it.

This may be a hang-up I've developed from 'My Worst Round Ever' (page 146) but more of that later.

Bad Luck Old Boy

It's considered bad form to laugh when your playing partner hits a monumentally bad shot. No matter how much the temptation. Majestic slices into trees, fat fluffs into lakes, dribbly duffs as far as the ladies' tee can seem quite hilarious, especially if you know the player. My favourite of all is the putt that goes speeding past the pin and off the green and thus ends further away from the hole than it started. There is a kind of hilarious pathos about this situation.

Similarly, when golfers chip uphill onto a fast sloping green and don't give the ball enough momentum, it can come rolling back down towards them and settle mockingly at their feet. This often happens at the Masters where the greens are so slippery most balls need crampons to stay attached to the putting surface. This is a joy to watch. Seeing a well-paid professional execute a shot so badly you could have done better yourself is thrilling to behold.

When they play a complete hole badly with the kinds of errors of judgement that you take onto the golf course every round, i.e. wrong club, wrong shot, wrong approach, wrong execution then it is mesmerising. The patron saint of crap golfers is Jean Van de Velde who had the Open Championship in his grasp on the 18th hole at Carnoustie. Had he just played the final hole like your average 24-handicapper he would have won. Greg Norman blowing up against Nick Faldo at Augusta in 1996 and converting a five-stroke lead into a six-stroke loss is similar. This is the kind of thing sports fans remember, not finishing par-birdie-par to take the win by four strokes.

Practice Swings

You're not really supposed to take a divot when you try a practice swing. Especially if you're putting. Come to think of it, you shouldn't really be taking a divot when you hit the putt for real...

On the tee you can practise your swing on surrounding semi-rough, or when you're standing up there between the markers, you can go through a low-speed version of your swing. But it's considered bad form to try a full-blooded practice on the tee.

I once played on a public course in Sussex with a golfer – and we've probably all witnessed this – whose practice swing bore no resemblance whatsoever to his shot swing. For his practice he was elegance itself: lovely takeaway, took the clubhead back in a perfect movement. He turned at the right time, swept the club downward and through, a pleasure to watch.

For his real shot it was like someone had flicked a switch and substituted a Chuckle Brother. His swing was rushed and jerky, he threw his body into it, and it was a lottery where the ball went.

He was a complete stranger so I didn't feel I could broach the subject directly – and besides, I was winning. However, towards the end of the round curiosity got the better of me and I asked him if he'd ever seen videos of his swing, mentioning quickly that I'd found it tremendously helpful. He replied no, he hadn't. He was worried if he over-analysed it he might start doing something different, "and my game would go to pieces."

Shouting Fore!

This is something that beginners learn fast. When errantly dispatching a hard object towards a fellow golfer at great velocity it is only polite to alert them to the fact that they could soon be testing out one of Newton's laws of motion relating to equal and opposite reactions.

Invariably it's the more experienced playing partner

that yells the first "Fore!" while the novice golfer freezes in horror at what they've just done. From then on it has to be a steep and fast learning curve.

The reason that "Fore!" is shouted and not, "Hoy, I say! You there!" is that it is short, easily recognizable and you can get some lung power into it. It's thought to be derived from the shout "Forecaddie!"

In days of old when golf balls were the equivalent of £50 each and youths were cheap to hire, a gentleman golfer would send his forecaddie down the fairway to spot the ball. In these windy and blustery conditions (and especially on blind drives) they would be forewarned by the shout of "Forecaddie!" that eventually got shortened into "Fore!". Or if Natalie Gulbis is playing: "Fworrrrr!"

Fore Tales

My friend Tim tells me that his very first venture onto the golf course with his father almost ended in disaster after a nasty Fore! incident. A few holes into the round and the novice Tim was hacking along several yards at a time in the semi-rough. His father went off ahead to look for his own ball that had disappeared into the bushes. Then, for once, Tim actually connected with a shot. His pleasure at actually getting one away was curtailed by the fact that it was heading towards the area where his father was looking. Sensibly he yelled "Fore!" At which point his father stopped bending over, looked up and was struck on the forehead. He says he was grateful that there were other people on the adjoining fairway at the time.

Another friend, who asked to remain anonymous, says he once played with someone in a club strokeplay competition who deliberately failed to shout Fore! to a group of golfers that he missed by centimetres (his ball went out of bounds). When asked why he didn't shout a warning he joked that he thought it was more likely to stay in bounds if they were all standing upright when he hit them. At the time my friend thought this was a bit of inspired improv comedy, but by the end of the round he realised that the guy was deadly serious.

Bunkers

Beautiful British golf courses are sprinkled with hazards such as brooks, burns, lakes and bunkers. They don't have anything known as a trap. If you find your ball in a trap, you need to call out the pest division of Rentokill. If you find yourself playing with someone who calls a bunker a trap, you can still call out Rentokill but increase the dosage.

When your ball lands in a bunker and you manage to find your way out, good etiquette demands that you rake over all traces of your visit. To minimise the amount of work involved it's best to enter the bunker at the closest point to your ball. Now this might be a statement of the bleedin' obvious, but you'd be surprised how many people walk in from the direction of the tee.

Help is at hand, though. If your social life is a flatline you can actually spend time on a website that will take you through a step-by-step procedure of how to rake sand uniformly, leaving the bunker in a better state than when you arrived. It's the golf equivalent of a book on napkin folding. You can also click through to a separate page on the theory of where to leave the rake. No, really.

Pitchmarks

When you eventually get on the green, pretend you are in church. No, not in church on Christmas Eve for midnight mass when you've staggered out of the pub, and you feel like a bit of a singsong for Jesus – who actually was a really good bloke and had great ideas that we could all live by. Treat the green with the respect and reverence it deserves. After all, you should only be two strokes away from holing out.

When your ball landed on the green, chances are it left a pitchmark where it bounced. It's your duty to seek out this dented bit of turf and un-compact it with a pitch mark repair tool. Unlike stamping back a divot, repairing a pitchmark does have a consistently beneficial effect for your fellow golfer, though the former's done a lot more than the latter. I always get the sneaking feeling that I've repaired someone else's pitchmark. The only time I know for sure that I repaired my own was in a society Stableford at the Leatherhead golf club in December 1998.

I hit a superb steepling 8-iron, into the 9th green, probably the best I've ever hit (certainly making up for driving into a tree and then hacking out more or less sideways). It was a cold, wet miserable day and the greens were sodden. When I got on the green there was my beautiful ball, five centimetres from the hole and five centimetres away from a big fat pitchmark. Now that, I was certain, was mine.

The sad things was that my two playing partners had dalliances with the trees and both gave up on that hole not even bothering to attend the green, where I stood with my ball next to the hole like some prize angler waiting for the photograph to be taken.

Marking Your Ball

Once the pitchmark (and technically all the other pitchmarks you find, though frankly how long have you got?) is repaired it's time to give your ball a wipe and check there isn't mud or an unfortunate bee squashed against the underside. I say this only because it must have happened to someone, somewhere and the first rule of contingency planning is to 'blue sky' a few scenarios.

First you must mark the position of your ball with a coin or a special marker that once clipped onto the back of your glove but doesn't any more and delights in finding the least accessible place in your trouser pocket. The idea is to place this marker behind the ball when you pick it up and put it down. Not as some bandidos try – in front of the ball when you pick it up and behind the ball when you put it down.

As markers can deflect the ball, you will be obliged to move it off other players' putting lines if it's likely to be in the way. Though it's often much quicker to refuse and say, "you're never going to get that putt anyway." Being on someone else's putting line is normally quite useful as it will give you a 'read' for the hole, so move your marker quickly and then stand annoyingly behind them. (By a stupid technicality, this might be marginally against the rules).

Putting Lines

On the putting green you should never walk between other players' balls and the hole, no matter how useless they are at putting or how long they've taken to line up the putt. Logically you might be doing them a favour by having your spike marks deflect the ball towards the hole, but it's never really viewed that way at the time.

With two of you playing it's very easy to avoid walking where you shouldn't. It's when you're in a fourball that you have to start paying serious attention, especially when one or two of the balls are replaced with markers.

If you're attending the flagstick, or simply hanging around nearby, it's also considered rude to oblige another player to putt through your shadow. Or to make bunny rabbit shadow puppets very close to their line of the putt. In which case you need to reposition yourself so it falls the other side of the hole. But still don't tread on anyone else's line or the bears *will* get you.

After all four players have putted out whilst meticulously avoiding stepping on each other's lines, the next group arrive at the green and if it's soaking wet they'll have to putt through your heavy footprints which won't have disappeared in the five minutes you've been gone.

Tap Dancing Verboten

Golf courses may be arenas of despair and crucibles of pain, but there is the odd joyous moment when a long putt goes in and the euphoria and surprise overwhelm you. Whatever you do, don't dance.

It's considered very bad etiquette to try and emulate Michael Jackson's moonwalk on a putting green unless you're an American Ryder Cup player and you've just kicked some European guy's ass, in which case it's natural exuberance...

Attending The Flag

It takes about ten years of playing the game to work out what you can and can't do with a flagstick, so if you're new to the game let's shortcut the process.

• You can have a flag attended from anywhere on the hole. Yes, you heard it right, anywhere. If you really like wasting time, ask for it to be attended from the tee of a very long par-3. Then, when your playing partner trudges up there shout, "Oh, no, I've changed my mind, it doesn't matter!"

• You might not be arsed to wander over there, but you cannot leave the flag in the hole when you're on the putting surface, it has to be either out or attended.

• If you're off the green, best leave it in the hole as it's a useful brake.

And that's it, that's essentially all you need to know. If you hit the flagstick that's lying on the green then; stupid you. If you hit the person who's attending the flag then you've probably used your driver and not your putter. The rules of golf have a curious twist in that if the person who's attending the flag can't get it out of he hole in time, or pokes at the ball with it and successfully makes contact, then you're the one that gets the penalty for asking such a barmpot to do it in the first place.

Stand Away From The Green

Once your group has holed out it's good etiquette to leave the green in a timely manner. If you have a group following behind then there are many things you can do to enrage them; these include practising the putt you've just missed (several times till you make it), standing around marking your scorecards, lighting up a cigar, paying each other out on bets made on that hole, or even sharing a Werther's Original.

Playing Through

Slow play is the curse of the modern game and, like impotence, men choose to ignore it rather than face up to the fact: "I am a slow player." Perhaps this book might be a useful purchase to those with erectile disfunction, sorry, I meant, to those who are slow players. It can be bought as a well-intentioned gift with a handy Post-it note slipped into this page.

Here's a little clue to spot the tell-tale signs if you are a slow player. When you start your round of golf, does the group in front disappear within a couple of holes, while the group behind seem to be putting out while you're teeing off at the next hole?

When you're playing on your own do ladies fourballs catch you up? Do small plants begin to grow on the mud that is left on clubfaces before you get back to the clubhoue? If the answer to either of those questions is yes, then you are a slow player and you need urgent help. Either that or you should give up the game and seek a career in the civil service helping pass government legislation.

GOLF CART ETIQUETTE

Set The Controls For The Heart Of The Green

Despite a fundamental opposition to the use of golf carts for healthy golfers in temperate climates, I do accept they are suitable in the following circumstances.

- For the elderly
- For those recovering from serious illness; strokes, heart problems etc
- On tropical and sub-tropical golf courses
- On golf stag weekends

Given my laudable and principled stance against them, when obliged to use one, I have devised my own set of Grumpy Guidelines that should be observed. These, you may notice, undermine the established etiquette which I have quoted and come courtesy of an American course guide. The Grumpy Guidelines are based on theory that driving a toy car brings out the kid in us.

• **Never drive the cart within hazard boundary lines, close to bunkers, or within 50 yards of the green. These areas can be especially susceptible to damage by the wheels of golf carts.**
GG: Drive as close to the green as you think you can get away with. Don't drive into a bunker in case the cart gets stuck.

• **Never drive the cart through mud, on or off the fairway.**
GG: Stick your foot flat to the floor and see how much mud spray you can make. It shouldn't be muddy anyway – if there's mud about close the course to carts. Durrrr.

• **Never drive through casual water on any part of the golf course. The wheels of the cart can do serious damage to the turf, including leaving ruts and tracks in wet areas.**
GG: It's your duty as a grumpy golfer to make as much cosmetic mess as you can manage without being thrown off the course. Strike a bloke for foot-power.

• **Never go joyriding in the golf cart. In other words, don't act stupid! People do get injured in cart accidents.**
GG: What is the whole 18-hole journey if it's not one self-indulgent, flabby-arsed joyride. Sadly there's not enough power in them to execute a few F1-style donuts, but any stunt-driving trickery you can manage on the cart tracks is to be applauded. How high can a golf buggy leap? is a

question I'd really like to see answered.

• **At new courses you should always ask what their standard golf cart rules are, then also be alert for any signage giving specific instruction on cart routes.**
GG: As a visiting golfer you have the gift of ignorance. Use it wisely.

• **A "cart-path-only rule" is exactly what it sounds like: Keep your cart on the designated cart path at all times.**
GG: What cart path was that...? Where? Oh, is *that* the cart path...?

• **The "90-degree rule" means that the golf course is allowing carts onto the grass but only at 90 degrees from the cart path. In other words, don't drive the golf cart up the middle of the fairway from the tee to your golf ball. Stay on the cart path until you are parallel to your golf ball, then turn off the cart path and drive straight to the ball.**
GG: Now you don't want to be a major pedant here, especially in America, where the thrusting young colonists have graciously adapted our language with an adornment of wonderful new expressions – such as turning nouns into verbs, thus we get "to summit" instead of reaching the summit and "to medal" instead of winning a medal. When they say at 90 degrees, shouldn't they also say at 270 degrees depending on direction?

• "No Carts Beyond This Point" sign. Even if you are allowed to drive the cart on the fairway, be sure to observe these signs.

GG: Observe them, yes, then run the golf cart gently up against them to see if they'll fall over with a gentle bump. Then carry on as you were.

• If you need to drive the cart quickly around the course (maybe badly need to find a restroom, etc.), be aware of golfers you are passing by. If a golfer is about to swing or attempt a putt, slow down as you approach and stop the cart until the golfer has completed his or her stroke.

GG: Quick driving on a golf course should be the default setting anyway. You should see it as a combined discipline of rally driving with golf – i.e. golfcross. This piece of advice, if applied to a British golf course, would be completely unnecessary. There are so many rest rooms dotted around the average British golf course that the need to find one speedily is completely eliminated. Sometimes I think that British golf courses are just a series of toilets linked by tees, fairways and greens. Certainly that's the way dog-walkers view public courses.

To be strictly honest I've never see a permanent "restroom" on a golf course. A couple of builders' Portaloos and that's it. And you wouldn't want to rest in one of those for very long.

Golf Cart Extras

Some other important things you should remember:

• They are sensitive to what gear you left them in when you got out. My friend Paul was playing with a group of mates and found his ball just over the top of a steepish hill. He got out of the buggy, played his shot and was convinced he'd left the thing in reverse. When he got back into the cart he found his sudden jabbing of the pedal brought about not the intended backwards motion he'd been expecting, but instead a surprise forward motion. Gravity gratefully accepted this gift of a golf cart and the buggy started to tear down the hill at a limb-breaking speed at which point Paul decided he had to abandon it to its fate. Which proved to be a small tree. He said the golf club was very good about it and he didn't have to pay for the damage. However, this was related to me in front of his wife, so you never know.

• They never float – no matter how many drinks you've had, they will never turn into Chitty Chitty Bang Bang and make a shortcut across the lake that guards the 17th green.

• They make rubbish getaway vehicles. Welsh rugby star Andy Powell hit the headlines in 2010 after he was arrested at a service station on the M4, having taken a golf buggy from his luxury hotel at 5.30 in the morning. Presumably he'd got a food craving for something stale and cold and decided to become a star in a reasonably underpowered car. His mistake was to fail to tell police that he was involved in some wacky golf marathon from Cardiff to St. David's in 10,000 shots and must have dropped his golf bag somewhere on the hard shoulder. Occifer.

RULES, RULES, RULES

Mulligan's Wake

If you didn't know (and I didn't know for a long time) a complete duff off the first tee can be discounted with a mulligan. It's a get-out-of-jail-free card that allows a golfer to replay his shot without penalty.

Mulligans don't apply in any of the PGA approved competitions such as The Open, The Masters or the Chesterfield and North Derbyshire Mixed Stableford. In fact, they should be banned altogether. Mulligans signal the decay of the moral fabric that holds our society together. If you can't stand the pressure of driving off the first tee then tough. How are you going to learn anything in life if there's an excuse every time you do something wrong?

Not content with having one mulligan off the first tee, golfers have started to invent more uses of them; a rolling mulligan that can be used once every round; two mulligans per round, one on the outward nine, one on the homeward nine. This leads golfers to bend the winter

53

rules so that they can claim a preferred lie from October through to April. My brother claims he knows a man with his own sign that says 'Winter Rules Apply' and posts it surreptitiously on the first tee just before his round. His surname's probably Mulligan.

Cink Sunk

Professional golf is one of those rare sports where the participants like to beat themselves up with a kind of rules masochism. Open Championship winner Stewart Cink was disqualified from a tournament for the most unbelievably mild of offences that brought him no advantage whatsoever. He hit a shot near the edge of a bunker that required him to stand with one foot in the bunker to play it.

Being a diligent player, after his shot, he asked his caddy to rake his footmark out of the bunker. When he got down the fairway he realised he'd put his awkward stance shot right into a bunker this time. But, he had already disturbed the surface of another bunker on that hole – "testing a similar hazard" – by the action of courteously raking his footmark. He should have given himself a two-stroke penalty and because he had only enquired about it afterwards he was disqualified.

I mean, how stupid is that. Not of Cink, but of the inflexibility of the rules. He got no advantage, was doing his fellow professionals a favour by raking up the footmark, yet the result is ejection from a tournament. He would have had a much better idea of the sand by standing in the bunker.

Contrast this with professional football where the participants – such as Thierry Henry – can score a crucial goal after deliberately controlling the ball with their hand. Henry's goal was allowed to stand because the referee didn't see it and it put Ireland out of the World Cup.

Sign This, Padraig

Signing for wrong scores in closely monitored and highly televised golf tournaments is another needless bit of self-flagellation. Padraig Harrington got booted out of the Benson and Hedges International tournament in 2000 for failing to sign his card. He was the overnight leader at the time. There was no attempt to cheat, the leaderboard was correct, it's just that a tiny signature on a piece of card was missing.

Instead of giving Padraig a friendly verbal cuff about the ear: "Ah, go on, you old rogue," they threw him out of the tournament. While you can see the necessity for doing that with the bandidos of club competitions, it's slightly different when you've got the world's sporting media following your every twitch and Ken Brown plodding along 50 yards behind murmering, "I don't think he can see the pin from there, Sam."

If the Royal and Ancient want to enforce ye olde ancient orders of golfe why not insist that professionals make their own golf balls before each round? That might keep Tiger away from the adult channels.

What's My Line?

If simple errors, such as failing to sign a card can have you thrown out of a tournament, how do you explain to the non-golfer what happened at Brookline in 1999? The Ryder Cup was on the brink of being won back by the Americans in an atmosphere not unlike the small disagreement we had in 1776 when we told them they had to pay for stuff.

Justin Leonard was playing Jose Maria Olazabal and was 45 feet from the hole with Olazabal a mere 18 feet away. Leonard sank his putt and the American players went crazy, racing onto the green and hugging him. They thought they had won, but Olazabal could still tie the hole. The penalty for touching or interfering with the line of putt is loss of the hole in matchplay. Why wasn't that enforced? Also (for those who have the video) why didn't they get deducted strokes for those shirts? I don't mean to cast aspersions about our American cousins' mode of dress, but if they wanted to look like Barbara Dickson why didn't they get the earrings and the curly perm to match?

Grumpy Rules Masterclass

Question: My ball is stuck in a tree – what are my options?

Answer: How on earth would you know? Unless you chipped it straight in there from about 50 yards. Most golf balls hurtle into trees at a considerable mph never to be seen again. The idea of lodging the ball in a tree is about as likely as succeeding in that toy game where you have to balance all those little ball-bearings in individual holes…on a cross-channel ferry…in a Force 11 gale…while drunk…and holding a kebab in the other hand.

For a start you have to establish that it's your ball before you play it, so a small white object half way up a tree might be yours or it might be someone else's.

Bernhard Langer has successfully played out of a tree, but few others. Many more have successfully played while out of their tree, but that's another story.

Question: What happens if a colour-blind squirrel mistakes my ball for a large, Titleist-sponsored acorn?

Answer: You always have to play the ball where it lies. Thus any outside agency such as a dog, rabbit, magpie, alligator or crow can mess up a really good shot. If they happen to bear a grudge against you, then they could follow you from hole to hole and ruin your whole round.

I'm surprised no-one has trained a Yorkshire terrier to improve their lies where there is a blind drive or blind shot to the green or on a – wait for it – dog-leg. True, it might be slightly suspicious if you had a ball that smelled of Bonio but it could gain you four or five shots a round.

It's the same with spectators – who can forget that round at the World Matchplay championship back in the past, when some player or other (probably British) hit his shot too long over the back of the 17th green (or it might have been the 12th). The ball trickled downhill into the spectators and then several seconds later defied Newton's law of motion and came bouncing back up the slope and onto the green.

Good Rules To Ignore

Rule: If a ball is lost or out-of-bounds, the player MUST go back and hit again from the point where the last shot was played (one stroke penalty). If you lose your ball on your drive, you must return to the tee (and may re-tee the ball) to play your third shot, etc.

Practice: What? And let the annoying pair behind through while you do it? No chance. The rule here is to drop a ball very close to where you think you drove it to – and you're there for three. Sorted.

Rule: You cannot improve the position or lie of your ball, the area of your intended swing, or your line of play by moving or bending anything growing or fixed, or moving or pressing anything down with your club or foot.

Practice: You can bend anything and everything as far as you like providing you don't break it off or move the ball. As a nature lover you're allowed to interact with your environment.

Rule: You cannot drop a ball along the imaginary line known as the "line of flight."
Practice: Yes, but it's so tempting.

Rule: You cannot ask what club a fellow competitor or opponent used.
Practice: What is this – a convivial sport or The Stasi? It's plain rude not to comment on a fine shot by an opponent and you can hardly say – "what a fabulous anonymous-iron that was".

Golfers Who Know The Rules

There is always something mildly suspicious about a crap golfer who has an encyclopaedic knowledge of the rules of golf. I'm a big fan of playing to your ability and knowing the rules to your ability. It's okay for scratch golfers to know detailed subclauses – of what to do if the person attending the pin gets struck by lightning and fails to get it out in time.

There's something a bit insidious and wrong about knowledgeable crap golfers – like teenagers who want to become football referees instead of playing the game on a

Saturday afternoon. Unless they're female referees in which case it's just wrong, wrong, wrong.

Boring Course / Interesting Rules

Some golfers are condemned to play on courses that are so boring a high percentage of the members develop narcolepsy. A friend who plays regularly on the infield of a famous race course (18 holes, three bunkers, one tree) has invented all kinds of weird rules to make things more interesting:

• Three club rounds – usually a driver, a 7-iron and a putter

• Left-handed putting

• Left-handed par-3s

• Blindfolded driving (when in a fourball and your partner can line you up). Each duo takes the better drive

• Driving on your knees like Toulouse-Lautrec. Not great etiquette admittedly, but there's nothing in the rules that says you can't adopt the stance of a famous French post-impressionist

• Playing matchplay for golf clubs. Every time you win a hole you take one of your opponent's clubs. Theoretically this could last only 14 holes.

TRICKY LIES

Verandahs

There's a bit of the Severiano Ballesteros in all of us.
Seve's ability to get down in two from almost anywhere
around a green endeared him to millions. We all want to
be like Seve and make that impossible chip or the
improbable pitch that leaves the merest tap-in to save par.
You can count my brother-in-law in with this merry
band. He put his ball onto the verandah of Woking golf
club and on finding that it wasn't technically out of
bounds, decided to chip back onto the green. The good
news for him was that in October it was hardly being
used. It's awkward enough getting spectators to move
their position on a golf course in a tournament, but
getting people to change lunch tables because they're
blocking the line to the pin might seem to be a bit bossy.
He didn't get down in two.

Cow S**t

During my college days I played a few public courses in
rural Scotland with a friend who was at Edinburgh

University. They were a lot different to the courses I was used to in the south. On one, some of the fairways were being grazed by cattle with the greens roped off. This led to the inevitable problem of a ball landing in cow dung. And we kind of wanted it to – in a *Jackass* way – so that we could say we'd played out of "a really crap lie". I don't think I'd have been keen if it was dog faeces. I'd done rabbit before, but everyone's done rabbit.

The excrement I drove into wasn't your archetypal cow pat like a medium-sized deep pan pizza, it was more strung out, as though it were deposited at speed – on the hoof. My ball was found nestling up against it. The pat couldn't be moved because it was solidly attached to the ground. The consistency was brittle, like a crust of a slightly burned school pie. I hammered a hooking 7-iron through the green amid an explosion of pat-bits all around me. I have to say, it wasn't a life-changing experience. Just like a big smelly divot really. Fifteen years later I could still smell it in the grooves.

For rules fans who want to know the ruling about droppings, they have to be treated like twigs or other natural loose impediments. There's no free drop. If you splat into it, or just attach lumps to your ball, it's like mud, it becomes part of the ball. Should you score a bull's-eye on a cow pat, the whole cow pat becomes a part. In which case it's probably best to declare that it's an unplayable lie. Cow pats are notoriously bad for distance and backspin.

Water

Water comes in three forms on the golf course; in a water hazard, in a lateral water hazard or at the 19th hole with whisky. And then there is casual water, which can be every grumpy golfer's joy because it means a free shot. One thing unifies them all though and it is this: Shots out of water are pretty pointless. When you've enjoyed the heady splendour of striking a ball through the excrement of highland cattle or played shots out of your club car park (gravel, not tarmac), a bit of water is neither here nor there. Most of the time your ball's disappeared in too deep or you can't swing a club at it. Or if it's near the surface of a brook, then it's stuck between two pebbles and any proper swish at it will re-engineer your Cleveland wedge to such a degree that any claim to be precision forged will have been superceded by the shape you've bent it into. It's only very rarely that it nestles on the edge of a brook inviting you to hit an ill-judged shot and get wet for your troubles. People can so easily mistake the splashmarks on your trousers for a hasty trip into the woods.

Even Jean Van de Velde thought better of playing out of water at Carnoustie in 1999 when he took his disastrous seven on the 18th. He did everything wrong on that hole but even HE conceded that it was a waste of a shot playing out of water (and he knew how to waste them).

Casual Water

There are lots of definitions of casual water depending on whose publication you read, but the one I prefer is: water that is a lot more relaxed than formal water. Casual water is a "temporary accumulation of water" on the playing surface whether it be tee, fairway or green. It can be as small as a puddle or as large as three holes entirely underwater after the river next to the course bursts its banks. It's hard to think of a river in flood carrying tree trunks and dead cows along with it as casual, but the Royal and Ancient would consider it so. Provided it was outside the marked stakes of being a lateral water hazard. The rules of golf are detailed in the extreme and no doubt there is a ruling for what happens if your playing partner gets swept away in a raging torrent. It would be a shocking situation to contemplate should such a disaster occur – there would be nobody to sign your card.

The English Channel As Casual Water

One of the hardened band of nutters who like to play golf wherever they can, thought it would be a fabulous idea to make three holes out of the Goodwin Sands in the English Channel. The Goodwin Sands have always been a tricky lie but mostly for shipping and especially for

U-Boat *U-48* which went aground there at high tide in 1917. (They had to hole out with scuttling charges). At low tide there is enough space for three holes, but a lot of the fairway and green gets washed away when the tide comes in, thus making the English Channel the biggest stretch of casual water in the word. Golfers are entitled to take relief from casual water, but they'd probably have to take it in Folkestone. Not ideal.

For the Love Of Two Centimetres

Grumpy golfers, rather than being depressed by casual water, see it as a great opportunity to get a better lie. All they need to do is take up their stance and find water emerging from the sodden ground around their feet to claim casual water. You don't have to find your ball in a big fat puddle, if the ground is 'casually marshy' that will do. Survival expert Ray Mears, using his back-to-the-wild techniques, can probably produce a pint of clear water from a small divot, so he'd be a brilliant golfer for free drops.

Now if your ball is immersed in the stuff then it's pretty obvious you can take a free drop. Which means you can gleefully alter your line to the pin, or if you're on the green, find a less tricky route for your putt. Though it hardly makes much difference to the shot you subsequently play, the joy is in the sheer anarchy of it all. Being able to abscond somewhere else with you ball is like officially truanting from school. The rules of golf are so oppressively rigid and inflexible, this is the one part where you get to interpret the conditions of the course and it's two fingers to the rules committee.

Snow

It's possible to lose a ball in casual water because nobody really is that keen to go wading into six inches of pond water that's accumulated on a fairway and spend the rest of the 14 holes squelching round with soggy socks. You may be able to see a ball nestling in there, but how do you know it's yours? And if it's not yours, then surely you've lost your ball? There's a whole slew of rules and case law about what to do in such circumstances. I say case law because you need to have "reasonable evidence" that your ball went in there to declare it lost. It's a situation that rules geeks love to bat backwards and forwards between themselves and, like train spotting or aeroplane spotting (with or without long periods spent in a Greek jail for spotting their two air force jets), it's about as interesting.

Another good area of casual water to lose your ball in is snow. Snow and ice are deemed to be casual water, unless it's one of those extreme golf courses (featured in the excellent *Extreme Golf* by Duncan Lennard) you get in the Arctic Circle where the whole course is snow and ice and hence casual water IS the hole. There is a Word Ice

Golf championship traditionally held in Uummannaq in Greenland around February or March. Each time they hold it they carve a new course out of the ice so competitors never get bored despite the colour. The championship includes rules such as being allowed to sweep your putting line clear of snow and driving between "fairways" marked out with flags. In the last two years it's been cancelled because of a lack of ice, which raises a problem unheard of in normal golf, i.e. your ball ending up on casual land.

Car Parks

Car parks can make for interesting lies providing they're not out of bounds. It's a crossover form of the game somewhere between crazy golf, urban golf and R&A golf. I've found it's best to be surreptitious about what you're doing when you play a shot out of a golf club car park, in case you get blamed for a dent that someone failed to notice then pins on you.

The Trickiest Lie Of Them All

The trickiest lie of all is when your wife finds a £300 charge on your shared VISA bill. I've run through all kinds of variants – it's for the Hurricane Appeal, helping underprivileged children learn to play golf etc.

I don't believe him for a second, but a friend of a friend said that he knew someone who told his wife that "Big Bertha" was a hooker in Amsterdam, because he knew it would go down better than being caught spending more money on golf.

FUN AT THE DRIVING RANGE

Fulfilling Something Primordial

Men have an urge to play golf. Perhaps it dates back to the stone age and the need to wield some kind of club hunter/gatherer style, but it's there. There are various ways men can satisfy this urge – playing golf on the Wii, going to the golf course or finding a driving range.

Driving ranges are singularly masculine places. Whereas women find their way onto golf courses – no matter what barriers you put up – they rarely make an appearance at the driving range. Those that do probably have significant testosterone levels.

I've often thought that the atmosphere you get in driving ranges is similar to walking into a large men's toilet. You walk in, take a look around. There's no chat going on, everyone's stuck in their own compartment getting on with their business. And it's a serious, solitary business. As you pass by you're largely ignored, but some people might peer at you before quickly resuming what they're doing. You find a free booth. Put your clubs down. Now, time to get your balls out.

Professionals At Driving Ranges

You always get the feeling that the people serving you at golf driving ranges wish they were somewhere else. I don't know what it is, there is that tinge of melancholy and regret in their demeanour. A feeling of: "How did I end up here doing this? I should be out in Valderrama warming up for the PGA event, not handing out buckets of balls to people who couldn't hit the sweet spot if it was the size of Leicestershire. A sigh is never far from their lips. Should Chekhov have written in the 21st century then surely he would have set a play at a golf driving range. You don't get that at crazy golf kiosks.

As a youth I'd go to the Lower Wick driving range in Worcester and spend an afternoon trying to slice 200-yard drives over the netting to hit the people on the pitch and putt course. The guy in charge was an old pro whose surname was Moses who had been the professional of one of the Worcestershire courses, but had to take this job on while his course was redeveloped from a 9-hole to an 18-hole course. Something happened which meant he couldn't return there. There was a court case and the *Daily Telegraph* ran a sub-editor's dream of a headline:

Moses Sues Over Promised Land. He was a nice old boy, togged up in tweeds most of the time, handing the balls over with old school courtesy. But he belonged in a smoky wood-panelled clubhouse with leather wingback chairs and plaques on the wall stretching back to the 1880s – not a Portakabin next to the water works.

Japanese Golfers

If you ever needed to find a Japanese national in a hurry the first place you should look is the driving range. The venue I currently favour for my remedial 3-wood blasts is a regular little hang-out for them. On Saturday afternoons there are often four of them in an enclave, pounding the Srixons into the wide blue yonder. Not aimlessly like the Brits, no, in accordance with a detailed practice schedule. They feel duty bound to keep at least one member on the premises at all times.

Children At Driving Ranges

I wasn't doing enough with my daughter so I suggested she come to the driving range with me. I was expecting her to say no. She'd been round a course with me on holiday before and got really bored, but picked a lot of flowers. When she said yes I imagined she'd be complaining after five minutes and wanting to go home.

Not a bit of it. When you take your daughter round on the golf course, she doesn't get to study other golfers' swings and shots in such fascinating close up. They're normally quite a distance away.

"That man's rubbish!" is the first thing I heard as she stared over the partition at the man next to me who was hammering away at the carpet.

"Shhhhh."

"No, he is! He is RUBBISH. He's hit three fluffs in a row. He's even worse than you."

I wanted to catch the guy's eye and give him a friendly shrug, you know the kind of thing, "kids huh, they say embarrassing things", but he stared resolutely at his ball and kept on fluffing.

So before she could say anything else I had to take her quickly aside and tell her it was rude to comment out loud about other people's shots. Even if, for some inconceivable reason, they *were* worse than mine.

Since then, whenever she comes with me I find the furthest position away from other people. She'll occasionally wander off to perform her David Leadbetter role with some of the less proficient players, but she tends to keeps her thoughts to herself.

Hitting The Golf Ball Retrieving Vehicle

This is one of the big attractions that driving ranges seem to have phased out. Many years ago, when golf balls were still relatively expensive, driving ranges only invested in a limited number of balls. On a busy day, when the cash desk was running low of balls, they'd send out the recovery vehicle to harvest some and bring them back. This vehicle was basically an old car with lots of metal grilles smothered all over it for protection, towing something that looked like a gang mower which scooped the balls up.

The minute it took to the range, it was every golfer's cue to zero their sights on the car and try and hit it. There was no harm to be done as the driver was fully protected and would merely hear the odd successful bang every once in a while. (And perhaps even a faint cheer). It added a new facet of 'rapid fire' into a staid game and was loads of fun. And it made you use a lot more golf balls.

(Nick Faldo wouldn't have liked it because he wouldn't have been able to get a shot away before the vehicle was safely back behind the kiosk.)

Presumably there are now Health and Safety laws that ban driving range employees from placing themselves inside a metaphorical duck in the shooting gallery, but I for one would welcome their return.

Perhaps somebody should introduce a mechanical target that crosses in front of the tees every 15 minutes or so, like they have on army shooting ranges. For people who've played on public golf courses I would suggest a cut-out of a dog-plus-dogwalker, woman on horseback, followed by a mountain biker and a pack of ramblers (led by a toothy bespectacled rambler).

The Fluff / Duff Recovery

There is always the temptation to go and recover the ball that has dribbled six feet from the tee and hit it again. My daughter, who has no shame (just like her mother) and now has her own junior set of clubs, has no compunction in getting balls that have gone that distance and slighty further. It's like coins in a fountain – free money. To many adults, this would be shameful. For a start you're owning up to the fact that you're the one that hit it that miserable piddling distance. You're also admitting you're a bit of a cheapskate. Pride can be an expensive sin on a golf course.

Machine Conspiracy

On the subject of being parsimonious, I always get the feeling that the golf ball dispensing machine is trying to cheat me in any way it can. I always come away with the feeling, 'that doesn't look like 100 balls!' But I'm always too lazy to count them.

Automatic Tees

The latest golf drive ranging technology is a fabulous improvement on the old wire basket of balls. For those who haven't seen one, you tip your balls into an underground hopper at one end of the tee, then close the lid. It then churns around for a few seconds, digesting the balls, then it regurgitates them mechanically, feeding them one by one into position on a tee for you to have a swipe at. You hit the ball, the tee disappears downstairs and comes up with another ball. It's very impressive and it's not rattled by the fact that you've aimed your Big Bertha at about 95% tee and 5% ball. It must have the same quality of glue that restrains Sir Elton's hairpiece.

The automatic tee height is adjustable, so you can go from a super-jumbo driver to an effete little pitching wedge.

It's great for hitting tee shots, but not so good when you want to hit it off the deck. Or maybe that's a button I haven't found yet.

It also lies to you about how many balls you've hit. After you've hit what seems like 36, it'll register 43. It's clearly in league with the ball dispenser.

Taking Automatic Tees A Stage Further

Surely the Japanese or Koreans must be doing this already, but you can imagine a driving range of the future that tracks each shot and gives you the data analysis on a screen installed on each booth. You'll get distance of shot, trajectory, degree of draw or fade.

You punch in the club you're using, then after you've finished, you could print out a multicoloured map, each colour attributed to a certain iron. It would be like one of those overhead maps of cricket shots where they show you if a player is strong on the off side or the leg side and in which directions he gets most of his runs.

We've all kept scorecards from blinding rounds of golf we've played, if only to convince ourselves of how good we once were, so this would be a very useful keepsake. In fact it could be a useful addition to driving range income.

Maybe Take It A Stage Further

How about going upmarket and having a few enclosed boxes at one end of the line of tees. Installed in your booth would be a machine that analyses your swing and tells you where you went wrong every time you hit an errant shot. It would show you a 3D trace of your swing with a superimposed swing on top demonstrating what you should have done to hit the optimum shot.

Add to this some vocal feedback, a bit like a golfing satnav system, "keep your hands further forward" and you could have virtual golf tuition.

This is for the keen monkeys of course. For the more leisurely minded of us, who know that identifying what you're doing wrong is one thing, and putting it right is a whole different ball game, then you could have a virtual commentator instead. For every shot you get some kind of feedback – "Great shot, was that really a 5-iron?" or "Wow, you blew the cover off that one, buddy!"

You could have a dial which ranged from 'Obsequious' at one end of the scale to 'Abusive' at the other. Thus when you scuffed a drive for 60 yards along the ground, at one end of the dial you'd get, "Ah bad luck, that was a tough shot to pull off." Or "You twonk, call yourself a golfer, my granny could have hit that further with one end of her Zimmer."

I'm off to the Dragon's Den for backing right now…

Shameful Wastes Of Time No.1

Two of the most laughable excuses for harnessing the 'golf urge', that unquenchable instinct to swing a club, are golf nets and golf course simulators. With a golf net you know very little about what's happened to the ball. You know if you've made full contact with the ball and you can tell the difference between a top, a shank and a fluff. But you have no idea what direction you just hit the ball in, whether it was a slice or a hook and you could be getting into the most horrendous of habits – all the while thinking 'wehey, that was a belter'.

Shameful Wastes Of Time No.2

The other waste of time is the indoor golf course simulator where you hit a golf ball at a screen and it estimates where you hit the ball to, before flashing up that position for your next shot. It's a fantastic simulation of the real thing. What could be more natural than swinging a club in a confined space indoors,

I am told they are a big hit on cruise liners, probably because the passengers are senile enough not to realise that it is a simulator, or the coffin dodgers love the fact that they can do even less walking than when they have a golf buggy.

If you look at the adverts for them on line they have the usual golf techno babble. Well, you can stick your digital artistry, your complex physics algorithms and precise 3D photography measuring spin axis, velocity and trajectory. I'm not interested in your proprietary immersive play vectoring. Three questions:

a) Downhill lies?

b) Uphill lies?

c) Bunkers?

Fun at The Driving Range

Yeah, not so clever now, are you, with your fabulously realistic simulation of real golf.

Horribly Real

Everyone knows that to simulate a proper round of golf you need to get stuck behind three black cab drivers, one of whom is so fat they make Angel Cabrera look like he could dance Swan Lake at the Royal Ballet. (Which I'd pay good money for anyway.)

Tiers Are Not Enough

The golf-crazy Japanese rarely get to play on a real golf course because there are only five in the entire country. (I think I've got that right.) All the reasonably flat land is used for building Toyotas and growing rice and the rest is mountains and bullet train. So instead they head to the driving range. But not any ordinary driving range, they have Golf-o-dromes, massive complexes entirely enclosed in netting with as many as four tiers from which to launch a ball.

Now you'd hope that they exercised some kind of differential pricing, because playing all your shots off the fourth floor of a building doesn't really give you much of a golf experience. So perhaps that's why the Japanese love British driving ranges so much – it's the luxury of turning up with your clubs and knowing that you're guaranteed a place on the ground floor. What's more, at one particular driving range in Surrey, a small girl will come round and offer an analysis of your swing, free of charge.

OLD GOLF CLUBS

Ah, The Auld Names

I have to confess, I'm a bit of an old club geek. Having started off playing with two I have an enduring affection for them. A chance was missed back in the....well whenever it was that someone thought it would be a good idea to replace the traditional Scottish names for golf clubs with the numbers of a matched set. How can a drive with a 2-wood compare with a great big thwack from a brassie? The spirit of Old Tom Morris was alive in the names of the clubs. Should your ball have ended up in a patch of rough grass 150 yards from the hole then that was perfect territory for a mashie-niblick. "I'll take a 7-iron," has no romance in it. Had we maintained an EU-like zeal for naming and renaming things we should have insisted that – like champagne – they keep their name of origin – or use both languages, like places in Wales. For those who hanker for a full run-down of what was what:

Woods

1 - Driver
2 - Brassie
3 - Spoon
4 - Baffy

Irons

1 - Driving Iron, Cleek
2 - Cleek, Midiron
3 - Mid-Mashie
4 - Mashie Iron
5 - Mashie
6 - Spade Mashie
7 - Mashie-Niblick
8 - Pitching Mashie
9 – Niblick or Jigger

There seems to be a glorious ambiguity and versatility about the use of the mashie. I had an old hickory-shafted club with a face that was pitched at about a 5-iron – which was probably a mashie – but you could angle the face over and use it as a 7-iron, 9-iron or even in the bunker. It was a lovely old club and I would still be using it for gentle pitch and runs had my kindly mother not given it away to the scouts when I was away at college.

Return To Hickory

Don't get me wrong, I'm not saying we should all drive Morris Travellers, drink our own cider and have an allotment, but golf could be greener. There's pressure on the world's water supplies, which golf courses drink up, and on the land space for those eager to grow their own crops badly and sit in a shed made up of mismatched packing crates.

There's also a problem in golf that new technology is making golf easier and golf courses shorter. One way to solve this would be to make everyone play with hickory shafted clubs again. That would cut the yardage down. And we need to start planning now. Should there be a sudden rush to hickory there won't be the trees out there. It'll be like when road salt runs out in winter and everyone blames the councils for not foreseeing that there would be the worst winter in 60 years.

We know that when economies emerge and their consumers get more sophisticated, they buy fast cars, drink more wine and start to play golf. Imagine what it's going to be like for Earth's resources when China with its one billion population starts embracing the Scottish Game.

That's why we need to start making golf more sustainable. Better to swap the graphite shaft for hickory now than be compelled to turn areas of semi-rough into a cabbage patch in the future.

Don't Stop At Bertha

We are returning to a more poetic and less accountant-inspired age for naming golf clubs. The introduction of the first Big Bertha was a milestone in that regard. But Callaway stopped short, they should have gone the whole 299 yards and named an entire set of golf clubs after women. Along with Big Bertha there should have been Subtle Sophie, a 3-wood equivalent that could be used off the tee or the fairway to shape shots. They could have had Awesome Anneka, a 3-iron (or driving cleek), Sweet Sue, a 5-iron equivalent with a large and forgiving sweet spot. For those vital short-game shots around the green, who better to have in your bag than the shortest female superstar there is, so rely on your Cute Kylie to get you up and down in two. An opportunity missed.

Rise Of The Hybrids

The great boom in club sales in the past 15 to 20 years has been the speciality clubs – the hybrids. Not as chunky as a metal-headed wood, but clearly more meaty than an iron, the hybrid club is a versatile little devil designed to get you out of trouble in the rough; thus they are often given names such as "rescue" or "recovery" or "launcher" (as if any golf club did anything else).

This is a bit judgemental. You might just like the club because of the feel or the balance and the way it swings. Thus you'll be obliged to rescue yourself from the middle of the fairway or recover from placing your ball on the tee of a tricky par three.

I used to play with someone who was married to their 4-wood and could hit it far more reliably and just as far as their 2-wood or driver. That 4-wood had all the small, neat-headed characteristics of a recovery hybrid. When he left it behind on the tee of a public golf course his game fell apart. That is, until he invested in a hybrid club. Now he rescues himself on 14 different tees in a round.

Up The Cleek Wi' Out A Baffy

Nobody is suggesting we go back to the auld Scottish versatility of a cleek, which originally was a shepherd's crook, but it's interesting to see that a lot of the old clubs were for getting out of trouble.

In the days before specialist greenkeeping staff, golf courses were a lot more like wind-blown sheep pastures than the genteel parkland setting of a Capability Brown design. Hence the clubs were more geared towards excavation than getting maximum backspin.

One of the clubs not mentioned in the list above was a "rake" which looked like a wedge but with several parallel slots cut in it to speed the clubhead through whatever the ball had landed in. This was designed for playing out of puddles and wet sand before the namby pamby days of casual water.

Similarly, there were a whole range of "spoons" designed for getting you up and out of trouble whether it be tussocks, heather or sheep output.

Choose Your Spoon

It was called the spoon because, like a spoon, it had a slightly concave face. There were five kinds (like I said – old club geek). You had your long spoon, for tussocky long grass. There was your middle spoon, which was shorter and stiffer and good for forcing a ball out of a grassy rut. There was your short spoon, which was used at about 8-iron distance, a baffing spoon for the same kind of shot from a fairway and a wooden niblick which varied from the mashie-niblick in that it was wooden. And like a wedge.

Which all goes to show that modern golf courses are pussies compared to what our ancestors had to put up with.

Golf And The Church

My local church likes to run posters on a noticeboard outside and they're always telling me why Jesus would be good for me. I would have to confess, his name does crop up from time to time on the average golf round –

especially at the long par-3 5th hole. Looking at the themes the church has run on its posters over the last few years they seem to specialize in forgiveness. Which is good. We all commit the odd sin or two and the knowledge that we might be forgiven for them is comforting.

Looking through the adverts in one of the golf magazines I noticed a hybrid club that apart from being used by top professionals, would deliver me "an optimal mix of performance and forgiveness". Which is also good. Knowing that you have a club in your bag that will not only give you great performance off the tee but will also forgive you when you hit the next shot out of bounds is surely taking club design to an uncannily metaphysical level.

It does raise more questions, though. Does it forgive every bad shot you make or just every shot you make with that club? Does it forgive bad putts as well? Will it forgive things beyond the golf course, such as opening your car door too far in the car park and denting the Jag you're parked next to. Has Tiger Woods got one? If so it's probably had a busy time of it.

Some New Old Names

Many golfers have heard of the mashie-niblick and the spoon, but the names of the other ancient clubs may well have passed them by. So you can have enormous fun inventing your own range of clubs and giving them stupid names – very much as Mizuno, TaylorMade, and Nike do with their own ranges today.

In my bag of auld hickory-shafted clubs handed down by Greet Uncle Reekie I have the following:

Spooter – For twaining off a tee when the wind's afore ye.

Hefting Spooter – For twaining off a tee when the wind's tae the rear.

Tossin' Spooter – For tossing behind a breeze wi' a mite bit o' loft.

Pitchin' Spooter – For tossing into a breeze wi' a mite bit o' loft.

Cleckin' Spooter – For all-purpose clecking.

Crummle – Like a 4-iron, only sharper.

Dredging Crummle – A thunderously heavy crummle for whackin' through a fair deal o' growth.

Pitching Crummle – A short-range crummle where you can tickle a ball up from 100 yards or less.

Tossing Crummle – Sometimes known as the steepling crummle, for lobbing a clear-lying ball high out of heather or a wee shitey spot.

Baffing Crummle – Like a baffing spoon, but with a crummle clubface.

And for bunkers I use a **wee graftie**

NEW EQUIPMENT

Precision Forged

There's an unusual dynamic going on in the golf showroom. The golf club manufacturers try very hard to persuade us to invest in new equipment knowing that we're suckers for anything that will give us a quick and easy advantage. It's not like football or rugby. You don't get Nike or Reebok telling footballers and rugby players that if they invest in their latest boots they're going to score more goals or make more tackles.

As monumentally stupid as they are, professional footballers realise that it's down to them to put the ball in the back of the net and not their equipment. Maybe it's us golfers who are the Br'er Bears of the sporting world. Because we see shiny new clubs, with futuristic designs, backed up by mock-scientific golf techno-babble and think ,"yeah, that'll put 40 yards on all my drives *and* straighten them up."

All we have to do is see phrases like "vector launch system" or "used by leading PGA professionals"or "low centre of gravity", "precision forged", "more workability and control" and we're convinced this will be the one thing that will finally get us that elusive Winter Stableford victory.

And they all mean absolutely spark all. Golf club design hasn't changed that much in the last 40 years. We had irons where you could move weights around in the clubhead and whippy graphite shafts back in the 1970s. We've moved from wooden woods to almost exclusively metal woods. We've had the emergence of the hybrid metal club to mimic some of the clubs of yesteryear, broom-handled putters, square-headed drivers – and what else?

Basically the job of selling golf clubs is by making the same thing we've had year in year out sound enticingly different. Manufacturers do this by buffing up their product in a different way. Common sense should tell us that 98% of the reason we hit a bad shot is because we're inept, the equipment shortfall was negligible. Most golf club makers claim any new clubhead has a sweetspot the size of Hertfordshire. But if you don't bring the club head down straight then you're only going to hit very sweet slices and very sweet hooks.

Key Words And Phrases

If you've got a new range of golf clubs coming out then you need many of the following ingredients:

• **Dynamic** – Golfers may be wearing beige crimplene slacks, but they like their clubs to be dynamic.

• **Consistent** – Next to 'power' consistency is a keyword that golfers look for.

Even though consistency has nothing to do with the club itself – you can normally rely on golf clubs to stay as golf clubs and not take Buddhist vows and reinvent themselves as cupcakes.

• **Adjustable Forgiveness TM** – all great golf club ranges need some kind of trademark concept that gives them that all-important air of exclusivity – a system that harnesses power, balance, energy, or control.

• Our own **Grumpy Range of Clubs** is headed by The **Grumpmaster DyFoPo TX7** driver. We're aiming for dynamic (DY), forgiving (FO) and powerful (PO) in a club that maximises workability with four separate adjustable quadrant weights, giving up to 25% extra forgiveness.

• **Enlarged sweetspot** – The trick is, you don't have to say what it's enlarged from. It's a bit like that advert that says "kills up to 99% of all known germs". If it kills only 2% then that statement is still correct.

• **Includes slice-correcting features** – But you don't have to spell out what they are; maybe it's an arrow pointing in the direction you should hit the ball.

Includes draw-correcting features – That arrow again.
• **Deep centre of gravity** – Well, who wouldn't want this. Deep is good surely, unless it's followed by the word "undergrowth".
• **For increased accuracy** – Get some lessons.

Putters

While I realise that I am going to be a crap golfer with or without expensive clubs there is one club in the bag which is worth paying a lot of money for – and by a lot I mean at least a tenner – the putter. The great thing about a putter is that you can actually try it out properly in the pro's shop and see what suits you best.

When extolling the virtue of a putter in adverts the makers feel they have to emphasize a "soft feel". Golfers are promised a "truer roll" more "feedback" and "better alignment".

What is this soft feel all about? I can understand Andrex toilet tissue wanting to give you a soft feel, but not a golf club. And what's this nonsense about feedback? You hit the ball and that's it. In the nano-second of contact between putter blade and ball, the putter doesn't tell you, "Woah baby! A little less force on this one I think," allowing you to ease up and lessen the blow – too late. The feedback you get is by seeing how far the ball has shot past the hole so that next time you don't give it such a monumental hoof.

But who's going to buy an expensive putter from a mail order catalogue without trying it first? It's all down to what your local store has in stock combined with your ability to read the carpet in the shop.

These days the majority of putter heads look like Imperial Fleet attack craft from *Star Wars*. You expect to hear some kind of death ray photon blast noise as the head strikes the ball. Throw one of those up in the air after an Open-winning putt (a la Jack Nicklaus) and you could actually kill your caddy or playing partner.

Balls, Balls, Balls...

One of the most worrying things I read in a golf blog is about the nature of golf balls, especially this line: "However, it's not just a matter of which brand you prefer, there are many different specifications to consider when finding the right ball for you..."

A lot of my golfing time is occupied by finding the right ball in the rough, let alone the right ball for me in the pro's shop.

What is the right ball for me anyway? I can tell you quite easily what the right brand is for me. The brand I prefer is the one that leaves me the most cash in my pocket without looking like a range ball.

The right ball for me depends entirely on what shot I'm playing and how badly my round is going. Although

I've railed against illusory technology in clubhead design, one of the major factors contributing to golfers hitting the ball longer has been golf ball technology.

These days you can go for low-spin, mid-spin and high-spin. Or you could opt for firm feel, mid-feel or soft feel. You also need to choose between two-piece, three-piece, four-piece or five-piece golf ball construction. Oh, and then decide what brand you're going to go for and if you like the sound of a penetrating high trajectory. That's after you've worked out if you're the golfer with a "slower swing speed".

I don't mean to drag this book down to *Carry On* humour levels but if you read the advertising blurb for golf balls, you could easily imagine they were describing condoms. Especially the bit about the soft feel.

...Balls, Balls, Balls...

The bewildering choice of golf balls that are now on the market make my brain ache.

Callaway reckon that 50% of the golfers that come to them to have clubs measured to fit are playing with the wrong ball. And that kind of statistic just plays on your mind.

They plant the seeds of doubt firmly in your head that you could be doing so much better if you were using the right ball. 'I might be having a great round, but what if I was using a three-piece ball with mid-feel and low-spin. Perhaps I would have driven over that bunker on the 13th…'

It was oh so much simpler in the old days – there were cheap balls like the Penfold Commando and there were expensive balls like a Titleist and that was about it.

Refurbish Your Balls

A lot of the top names offer them, but what exactly are they? I can understand the concept of a Lake Ball, (though I still can't imagine the equipment you'd need to harvest them on such a grand scale). I can understand the concept of a refurbished home or a refurbished computer with new motherboard and extra RAM; but how the heck do you refurbish a golf ball? Do they mean **washed**?

The Golf Glove

The worlds of pop music and golf rarely collide, but this one small golf accessory clearly inspired a multi-million dollar image for the planet's biggest former pop star. True, Michael Jackson's single glove tended to be diamond-encrusted and may not have given him that much extra grip on the club shaft, but his adoption of it was a clear homage to a game he never played.

You only realise the significant part a golf glove plays in your game when you forget to bring it. It's the

Cinderella golf accessory. You treat it badly, stuff it in your bag after a round. Then a week later you pull out this thing that looks like an old banana skin (albeit a five-fingered banana skin) strap it to your hand and away you go. Whereas the ugly sisters, which are the golf shoes, get lovingly cleaned and don't add any strokes to the round whatsoever.

Not A Golf Sale...?

Is there anywhere on the planet that sells golf equipment at full price? Trying to find somewhere that actually sells the clubs at the recommended retail price is one of those tricky tasks way up there with reprogamming your operating system in boxing gloves. Perhaps you can get stuff at full price in the pro's shop on the Royal Dubai golf club where nobody would want to be seen buying a club at less than full price.

As such, the signs that direct you to a Golf Sale are pretty meaningless – even furniture warehouses have less sales than yer average golf store. Occasionally you see some poor sod stood on a roundabout holding a big banner that proclaims GOLF SALE together with a directional arrow. They always look thoroughly hacked off with life and who can blame them. Saying that, they still look happier than the people who take your money at a golf driving range.

SPECIALITY GOLF

Crazy Golf

A lot of serious golfers avoid crazy golf like the plague. They're not averse to playing with other club golfers, obviously. But the conversation rarely arises when four blokes in a car are heading down to a public course in Sussex when one of them suddenly says, "I know, here's an idea from left field. There's a really good crazy golf course in Bognor Regis by the pier, let's go there instead."

And competition between four serious golfers would be fine. It's when a "proper golfer" is pitched against their wife and children that things get nasty. Because the proper golfer is expected to win and his wife and children get enormous pleasure out of him not winning and getting angry. Especially if it involves a fibreglass model of Bambi.

Crazy Golf Balls

Most crazy golf balls look like they were manufactured in the 1960s. They have the weary, faded patina of age. Not for them the glories of being spanked down the 18th fairway at Royal Lytham in the final round of the Open, or helping the European team complete another triumph in the Ryder Cup.

No, their life is in the trenches of golf, getting hacked around by kids, grannies, drunken youths and the odd grumpy golfer. Had they got access to a pharmacy they would overdose on painkillers and self-harm.

For them, the life of a driving range golf ball is something they aspire to, at least they'd be struck onto a surface they were intended for – grass – and not bounced between concrete walls and along tarmac surfaces painted green. But they are stuck with their lot, until one day they are struck with such force by a youth from Leytonstone showing off to his girlfriend that they bounce clear out of the crazy golf course, out into the road and escape into a drain. And from this weary care-worn world they are released.

The majority of them have long since ceased to be spherical and like Earth have subsided into an oblate spheroid. Add to that chips and cuts and you have a ball that is never going to roll the way you putt it. Already the serious golfer's advantage is whittled away.

Crazy Golf Putters

The *sine qua non* of the perfect crazy golf round is the perfect crazy golf putter. These are typically the hammer head type and look like they were mass-produced in Bulgaria around the time Lee Trevino was playing his golf. Pick one up and it feels like it was put together by a 12-year-old in a metalwork class, the clubhead usually has independent movement from the shaft. That's if it stays on.

Calling the bit of the shaft you hold as a "grip" is perhaps giving it a bit too much credit. It's a heavily split rubber sheath that smells like a dead cat and also has independent movement from the shaft.

The combination of putting an oblate spheroid with a metal stick to which is loosely attached a putter head does not put the serious golfer in the best of positions in which to exert his golfing skill and prowess.

But we've yet to come on to the psychology and tactics employed against him.

Psychological Warfare

"You're supposed to be good at golf, Daddy."

In our family games the psychological battle starts early. My daughter, as we've seen, has single-handedly undermined the confidence of most golfers at our local driving range: Apart from the outright, "that man's rubbish" she has a nice line in standing directly behind tees, watching, sighing and shaking her head gently.

Despite being the youngest in the family she is the most competitive and knows how to deliver the lowest blows. Standing on the first tee, facing the tricky ramp into the tunnel through the clown's head, with your crap ball and your wobbly putter, she'll start the war of words. Turning to the others she'll say in a very loud whisper.

"Wait for Daddy to blame his putter."

Or, before you're actually making the stroke she'll pile the pressure on, "This looks really easy Daddy, I bet you get this in one."

So, you muster all your concentration together, your specialist putting grip somehow bonds the frayed and skanky-smelling rubber to the shaft, you produce a beautifully weighted, straight putt and the freakily-shaped ball starts off arrow straight towards the tunnel in the clown's mouth. It's a triumph of skill over equipment. Then at the last second the ball hits a knobble, strikes the clown's fat red nose and then trickles back down the ramp to your feet.

"Bad luck, Daddy," she says, not meaning it for a second.

When you've finally holed out in eight, she steps up with her cricket bat grip – one hand on the top, one hand half way down the shaft and makes a loose swoosh at the ball. It heads two feet left of the clown's mouth, hits a knobble, goes straight through the tunnel in one and she putts out with a two. "This is easy," she smirks, upping the ante for hole No.2, the crocodile.

And so it begins.

Crazy Golf Holes

From a mental health point of view, my therapist and I have been working towards forgetting every crazy golf hole I've ever played. But in nightmares they keep looming out of the fog towards me.

There is one in the Austrian ski resort village of Kaprun which keeps coming back to me time and time again. For this hole you had to launch the ball up a ramp after which it jumped, *Dukes of Hazzard* style, onto a concrete island with a hole in the centre. Those of us who have seen the energetic way in which a golf ball bounces on a road will appreciate that concrete is not the easiest surface to control a golf ball on. You had to hit it hard to get it up the ramp, but unless you landed the ball on this one perfect spot with your tee shot it would bounce up, left, right, back at you with machine gun ferocity. I managed a 37, my wife did it in 29, none of the children finished it and my daughter lost her ball. Either that or it got dark.

I've had a similar experience with a motorised windmill, but that was just a case of bad timing. On this particular hole you had to time your shot so that it went through the door of the windmill, a bit like Windy Miller of *Camberwick Green* fame (but without the polystyrene smock). For some reason I kept on hitting the sail or missing the door and it got very infuriating, especially combined with the heckling.

That is something you don't have to put up with on a proper golf course; people jeering at you, pulling faces and singing theme tunes to old children's television series. Unless of course it's in America during the Ryder Cup

Crazy Golf Rules

My daughter's interpretations of the rules of golf are fluid and I have to say I admire her willingness to take the authorities on. Both her elder brothers were happy to play by the rules that I first suggested, which were more in line with the way the R&A think the game should be played – i.e. waiting for the ball to stop before playing your next shot.

My daughter's interpretation is more complex. She believes that this rule doesn't apply when the ball has passed close to the hole twice and should have gone in before now but for some reason hasn't. On the third attempt it's quite legitimate to knock it in on the move, providing you say, "It was going in anyway" and then stick your chin out.

Le Mini Golf

We all know what a mini bar is, but what is mini golf? Is it crazy golf but not that deranged? Is it straightforward putting? Is it pitch and putt? What's the deal here?

Mini golf seems to be a cover-all phrase used much on the continent and, unlike anything else witnessed in the regulation-hungry EU, there are no hard and fast rules for the length or shape of the hole – you can have bendy ones and straight – or what kind of obstruction you're going to find along the way. It could be a labyrinth of concrete blocks or a sunburnt, be-flipflopped German who's fallen asleep clutching his wurst right across the 14th.

Euro-Crazy Golf

Talking about the European Union, it might be a nice development for the EU beaurocrats, working their 23-hour week in Brussels, to relax of a three-hour lunchtime on a Euro crazy golf course. They could have a nationally-themed crazy golf course with each hole representing a nation. The Spanish hole could have snow-capped mountains to represent the Pyrenees, where you putt a ball up a zig-zagging mountain road, like the Port d'Envalira. The Dutch hole would be flat with a few big dykes either side, the Italian hole would pass under a model of the Coliseum, and the Greek's would have a big black hole to represent their economy. On the course you would go straight from the UK to Belgium missing out France whose hole would be closed due to unofficial strike action.

Pitch And Putt

Despite having pilloried crazy golf, it is still a much more acceptable sporting challenge than pitch and putt which is just bastardised golf with the wrong equipment played by a bunch of ASBO youths who would do better digging an allotment on a Youth Citizenship scheme.

Crazy golf doesn't attempt to mimic real golf, it's a separate entitity. Pitch and putt is as poor an introduction to real golf as Heathrow Terminals 1, 2, 3 and 4 are to the United Kingdom.

Whereas crazy golf course owners know that the participants are going to take chunks out the fairway and possibly the greens and construct them from appropriate materials such as tarmac, concrete or heavy-duty fabric, a pitch and putt course is far more vulnerable. It has to be made out of grass and consequently gets lumps taken out of it from endless dreadful shots and sometimes out of malicious intent.

The only thing that distinguishes a pitch and putt course from a playing field is that the fairway is one mower cut lower, and the tee and green are two cuts lower. The difference between the tee and the green is that the green has a flag in the middle and there are marginally less divots taken out of the green.

Like It And Lump It

Like crazy golf courses, pitch and putt courses arm you with an array of unsuitable equipment with which to tackle their unsuitable course. I once queried why I would need a 7-iron to pitch a ball 40 yards. "That's what you get," was the answer from the guy behind the counter who probably didn't go on to work for Mizuno.

The Saddest Sight In The World

There is nothing so sad as a faux bunker or a faux water hazard on a pitch and putt course. These are just thin scrapes in the ground, out of which all the sand has been hacked or all the water drained off. You can only tell the difference between the two by the fact that one has a slightly raised lip and one doesn't.

God knows what the 25th century's equivalent of Tony Robinson and *The Time Team* would make of them, or a pitch and putt course in general: "This was either a golf course for a race of dwarf-like people or for the young of the village."

Urban Golf

As we've seen from our detailed investigation of crazy golf, the golf ball, as designed and manufactured in the 21st century, is only intended to make an interface with one hard surface per shot and that's a clubhead. It doesn't behave all that well when it gets to strike a variety of hard surfaces. Especially glazed products.

Up until about 15 years ago, men's mags took the punk view that golf was like fishing with no sense of "cool" whatsoever. Then we got the impact of *Loaded* magazine which proclaimed golf to be funky, just because it had been so unfunky, and a new generation of golfers came through. Now we have stars like Justin Timberlake and the band Keane playing the game.

Part of *Loaded*'s championing of the game involved subverting it by playing in a landscape that was desperately unsuited to golf: thus we got Urban Golf. There is a *Jackass* mentality to playing golf when you're sober, in an environment where you can do quite a lot of damage. It's like attempting a stag night stunt when you're stone cold sober.

People hate golfers enough without inflicting urban golf on them.

Cross-Country Golf

The idea of cross-country golf dates back to at least 1898 when Mr. T. H. Oyler and Mr. A. G. Oyler accepted a wager that they couldn't reach Littlestone-on-Sea from Maidstone in under 2000 shots. They played alternate strokes and brought along an umpire to verify their progress. The normal rules of golf were said to have been applied for things like lost balls (all 17 of them) and they employed a succession of boys to act as caddies. They got to Littlestone in 1087 shots after covering 35 miles in three days. Hardly worth it for a fiver old man. Since then there have been many cross-country attempts, including one that went from the Atlantic coast of America to the Pacific coast and took a year. I find 18 holes frustrating enough but a whole continent...?

Crazy Golf Extended To Real Golf

You have to admit that when you've seen a lot of aerial photos of Florida golf courses in all their lush green manicured perfection you yearn for something different. So much of today's golf is a big drive followed by a steepling wedge into the green. They've managed to precision mill the grooves on clubfaces now that will give you backspin from the middle of a gorse bush, so the art of the chip and run is declining.

I would love to play on a golf course that changed

all that – where you have two massive oak trees in front of the tee and you have to shape a low drive underneath them. Or where you have trees protecting the green and you are forced to play a chip and run approach.

How about a themed golf course where holes are adapted to suit a variety of different landscapes and environments – like crazy golf on a massive scale? For an urban-themed hole you could have a fairway that is split by a canal into which have been pushed a dozen supermarket trolleys. The greens would be protected left and right by burnt out Vauxhall Zafiras.

Instead of a par-3 (water) island green you could have a Milton Keynes traffic island-themed hole. You tee off on one traffic island and play towards another. Now that really would be a Road Hole.

And of course, the saving grace would be that even if it didn't attract any members, it would probably get Arts Council funding or win the Turner Prize. And then Antony Gormley would want to add a hole with 500 naked sculptures of himself lining the fairway and call it 'Gormley' while claiming the hole was not about him at all but about the common man.

SUNDRY IRRITATIONS

There are many things that can irritate a golfer. Very rarely do things go 100% right all the way through 18 holes. Golfers tend to accentuate the negative and undervalue the positive. In a round where you scored a remarkable birdie on a long par-4, deemed the hardest hole on the course by the stroke index, you tend to remember the enormous duff you made on the easy par-5. Even days when God smiles on you, all you can do is think of what could have gone even better.

To emphasize just how impossible this perfect round is, let's embark on a tourist brochure kind of round.

The Perfect Round

• You arrive at the club and find ample parking – as it should be mid-week.
• The first tee is free and your playing partner is there on time.

- It's a beautiful sunny day, warm but not hot, with the gentlest of zephyrs sending a few catspaws over the lake guarding the 18th green.
- You hit your first tee shot and it's a cracker, neatly bisecting the first fairway and about 250 yards long. Two very fit lady golfers, who have paused for you to take your shot, smile admiringly in your direction.
- Your putt on the first green is beautifully judged and hovers on the edge of the hole for a tap-in for par. What a great start.
- "Well done," says your playing partner beaming with genuine appreciation.
- You continue on the front nine playing a series of inspired shots to achieve your best ever outward score.
- On the 11th hole you hit an errant tee shot that is hooking out of bounds when it strikes a giant oak tree and lands back in the centre of the fairway. You drill an iron into the heart of the green and hole a tricky, snaking downhill putt for your first birdie.

    The fit lady golfers in the match behind, both in their twenties and clearly lingerie models by profession, applaud.
- By the par-5 18th hole you are on the brink of your greatest round ever, but don't know if you should go for the flag and a birdie or lay up short of the lake. Even a five will put you eight shots clear of your greatest ever score. In a Nicklausian moment you take off your sweater but take too much turf with the shot. The ball is heading for watery ignominy when at the last moment a gust of

wind boosts it on and it lands safely on the fringe. From there it's an easy pitch and a roll in to finish on birdie four.

• In the clubhouse afterwards one of the fit lady golfers asks for your mobile phone number in case she needs someone to play a round with. (You knew that joke would get in somewhere and now the waiting is over).

The Imperfect Round

• Arrive at club to find almost no parking space at all. But it's the middle fo the week? Your heart sinks when you remember it's the Widget Federation Golf Society's annual golf match.

• The first tee is booked up and you have to start on the 10th.

• You journey out there and it starts to rain. You discover you left your golf umbrella and waterproofs in the car as the forecast had said "sunny intervals".

• You wait another 30 minutes for your playing partner to turn up and in that time two old bags in 1970s flares, who look like they've had cosmetic surgery in bulk and make-up applied by Barbara Cartland in the dark, abuse you for holding them up.

• Your first tee shot doesn't get as far as the Ladies' tee and they both look at you like you're something that should be scooped in the park.

• You get to just off the green in four and your fifth shot

is going to shoot straight past the pin and way off the other side of the green when it hits the flagstick and drops flukily into the hole for a bogie.

• "Well done," says your playing partner with barely concealed resentment.

• On the 11th hole you hit an errant tee shot that is hooking out of bounds when it strikes a giant oak tree and bounces straight out of bounds. You hit a second which does the same. Your third ball slices onto the next door fairway and the two old bags behind moan that they ought to be let through.

• You continue over the next seven holes playing a series of insipid shots to achieve your worst ever inward score to date. You decide nine holes will be enough.

• By the par-5 18th hole you are on the brink of your worst score ever. You are soaked to the skin and are regretting the over-loud joke you made to your playing partner about the harridans behind being "natural hookers". You're not stupid enough to go for the green and lay up short of the lake. Then your finely-judged pitch – the one good shot of the afternoon – gets caught by a gust of wind and goes plop in the lake.

• In the clubhouse afterwards one of the lady golfers asks for your mobile number because she is going to put you in contact with her solicitor. At which point you make it worse by saying, "don't you do your own soliciting" a remark that is overheard by the President of the Widget Federation Golf Society. When he tuts, you take a swing at him and it all gets very nasty...

Reserved Tees

We all know that clubs are desperate to raise finance and golf societies bring in extra revenue, but they're also a pain in the arse. You turn up to the course on what you think will be a nice slack day hoping for a rapid 18 holes only to find that the first tee has been reserved until a certain time. This means that there will be a juggernaut of golfers locked in a grim – but outwardly jovial and friendly – battle for dominance in their monthly bi-monthly or quarterly match. This slow-moving blockage will creep round the course with no obligation to hurry up because they are the customer and the customer is always right.

Club members are obliged to start at the 10th tee, and then when they get to the 18th green and try and start on the first tee, get caught up with the members waiting to go off the first.

Do players who have been directed to start on the 10th get priority over golfers waiting to start their round on the first? I've yet to find out.

Dogs On Golf Courses

Don't get me wrong, I love dogs. But on a golf course I love them very much as the Koreans love them – with fava beans and a bottle of nice chianti. They are one of two animals incompatible with a golf course – the other being a horse. Dogs aren't good because they think they have an obligation to pick up golf balls. Any spare ball lying around was surely left on the fairway for them to leave saliva on.

They also interfere with the natural lose one/find one scenario of hitting a ball into the rough. If you hit a ball into a tricky location, chances are you'll find some- one else's lost ball if not your own. When you've had a terrier go scampering through the rough, they hoover up everything not in sight.

On my most disastrous round of all time at Royal St. Georges, Sandwich, I arrived with seven golf balls, found another six en route, but had lost all 13 by the time I got to the 17th hole. (See *roundus horriblis* on page 146)

Had some zealous terrier been through the heather and gorse I would only have got as far as about the 11th which is when the seventh ball disappeared.

Horses For Courses

Horses aren't good because they don't like being stung by the sudden impact of a golf ball. Now if the riders were fat old country types in tweeds and breeches, or Jilly Cooper, it might be an interesting prospect to see if they had the rodeo skills to handle that situation. But as most horses are ridden by young girls or children, it's a worrying prospect and to be avoided. This isn't helped by the fact that many golf course have bridleways across them. Surbiton golf course, which is nowhere near Surbiton, actually has a stables located on a small island of land in the middle of the golf course, so heaven knows how they manage. Perhaps they never get out and they're all highly inbred (that's the horses).

Trolleys On The Green

As you know I'm not a fan of golf buggies. I tolerate golf trolleys but it's a grudgingly thin tolerance.

My friend Roger, who has recently retired from a long and distinguished career in the publishing trade, told me that he now plays with a seniors crew who are a remarkable bunch. One member, affectionately known as "the lad" is 82 and still carries his own golf clubs round. So if you can do that at 82 why do you need a trolley? Let alone an effete, motorised trolley, for the terminally limp-wristed.

For me, the motorised trolley is a symbol of our society's decay of standards. Golf clubs aren't that heavy. If you want to take round the full 14, plus umbrella, plus implement for fishing balls out of water, a ton of spare balls, hip flask (October to April), beer (May-September), waterproofs, spare glove and a selection of tees, and can't carry them yourself, then employ a caddy. We have enough youth unemployment in this country and the golfing indulgence is balanced out by the beneficial effect of spreading the wealth around.

Taking Your Motorised Golf Trolley Into Tesco's

How do the people who need motorised golf trolleys for golf ever find the strength to make it round Tesco's where they have to push the trolley themselves? That six-pack of Heinz beans weighs considerably more than a 6-iron, and what about the jumbo bottles of cola the kids insist on loading in? A couple of those on board and you're understeering round corners faster than Lewis Hamilton going straight on into the gravel. Perhaps the men who use motorised trolleys are all confirmed bachelors and shop lightly.

The Machismo of Trolleys

For these reasons, the moment I see a trolley encroaching on a green my grudging tolerance snaps and I become supremely irritated. Well, I'm often supremely irritated, but this drives me up to Defcon 1 (Or in grumpy parlance – Grumpcon 1).

There are many heroic images of sport: the beautifully timed late tackle in football, the try-scoring leap in rugby union, the nerve and sinew-shattering stroke of an oarsman in a rowing eight are all macho moments. A grown man pulling a golf trolley is not one of them. You can't imagine a slow motion head-on shot of four men pulling golf trolleys down a fairway as an image to promote a shaving product. Gillette – the best a man can get.

No, if a trolley is going to be used in any TV advertising it's for a Saga retirement scheme – some insurance or financial product that allows pensioners to live in comfort in the later years. Cue two old buffers pulling their trolleys down the fairway. Cut to one watching the other have an arthritic swing, then waving at them cheerfully, while desperately trying to remember what their name was.

A Ryanair View Of Golf

I'd like to see a Ryanair view applied to golf. The Irish carriers have pioneered low fares based on giving customers a standard fare and then getting them to pay for anything extra. So if you want extra luggage you pay more per bag. Why not apply this to golf?

Most golfers can get round a course comfortably with eight golf clubs – for me it would be 1- and 3-wood, 5-iron, 7-iron, 8-iron, wedge, sand wedge and putter. Make that the standard number.

If you want an extra club, that's an extra stroke on your score. So if you've got 14 clubs in your bag then you're already +6 for the round. Add on another two for a trolley, four for a motorised trolley and eight for a buggy.

Golfers Who Cut In

Like queue jumpers approaching a motorway contraflow, golfers who decide to start their round on the hole in front of you are pitiful scumbags for whom summary execution is more than they deserve. That torture with the fast-growing bamboo is probably what they do deserve.

Similarly, if you are enjoying a leisurely round, free of the hassle of another match right on your tail, and somebody jumps in behind you to put the pressure on, then that is similarly infuriating.

You might be playing a round with good-old-Phil who's a very entertaining bloke, but who takes four practice swings to hit the ball 70 yards. So you arrange to go off early to beat the 9am first tee rush and have just reached the seventh when somebody starts from the sixth tee and is instantly breathing down your neck. What started as an enjoyable day with an old friend is turned into a silent race where you are willing Phil to get a move on and all the while looking over your shoulder at the approaching pack behind. Though, that's still not as bad as a group who cut in in front of you and then proceed to hold you up.

Slow Play

Queues and congestion around golf courses at peak times are the bane of most golfers' lives. It's easy enough to understand why 'recreational' golfers can take a long time, hacking around, losing a ball here, losing a club there, getting stuck in a bunker for six shots etc, but professionals shouldn't take five hours to get round.

The problem with them is that they want free drops from everywhere. They hit the ball into a grandstand and they want a free drop. They nestle up to a TV cable, they want a free drop. If they can't have a free drop they want a ruling. What the R&A should do is make them play the ball from where it ends up. Grandstands aren't a surprise element to golf championships. No golfer arrives for the European Open at Valderrama and exclaims, (use Spanish accent here) "Dios mio! I did not suspect they would place a grandstand by the 18th green. It will have a magnetic attraction for my golf ball."

Spectators like the schadenfreude of a bit of professional humbling. After clattering the ball into a grandstand it should be up to the professional to find a route to the green, providing they haven't shot into some-one's rucksack (and even then that might be challenging) or plunked it neatly into a waiting thermos.

So many times you see pros muff it into the grandstands get a free drop in a lovely grassy area and get the ball up and down in two, when really what we'd like to see is a bit more pain for their error. If they'd fired the ball perfectly straight but short and into a burn, then they'd take a penalty, yet they can tonk it wildly left or right and get a pussy old lie for their inaccuracy.

Grumpy Rules: Chapter XV – Section 2.4

In professional competitions, free drops from grandstands will be from an area directly behind that grandstand. From a wooden pallet.

The Longest Day

The longest round of golf I ever played was on an August bank holiday Monday and it took six hours. What made this experience extra special was that by taking so long to get round the course I was forced to spend an extra hour in bank holiday traffic on the way home. Job may have been a patient man in the old Hebrew bible but he never had to use the M25.

Fidgety Routines

Golfers who have developed nervous ticks or fidgety routines before they can hit a golf ball also drive me wild. For a time I played with someone who used to shrug his shoulders and stretch his neck out, almost like a premeditated shiver before hitting the ball. We managed to curtail it by saying to him one time; "go on, do your Frank Spencer."

Poncey Putters

Meticulous putters are a nuisance when they're good, annoying when they're average, but actually quite hilarious when they're dreadful. There is something tremendously funny about watching someone go through all the pre-putt drill of a professional golfer, doing the old plumb-bob routine, pacing around with a serious look…and then stubbing it half the distance to the pin. True, the humour never lasts more than about six holes, but it makes up for having to play with them.

Token Bunker Rakers

There are some golfers out there who think that a golf club is an acceptable form of a rake and a few swishes with one and that's it, job done. Ask anyone who has an allotment if they use golf clubs to prepare the seed bed before sewing and you'll find that none ac·ually do.

Greenkeepers

I may be wrong about this, but in the past I got the impression that greenkeepers had an almost feudal relationship with the people who ran golf courses. The class system was alive and kicking on golf courses where they were considered the *untermenschen*.

For instance, you would never get a greenkeeper who was allowed to join in and play at the club. They were the hired staff and knew their place. They were like the gamekeeper Mellors in Lady Chatterley, but with a lot less sex and pheasants.

Today I'm sure they're viewed with the professional respect they deserve, not just as an entertaining target to hit while mowing a green and unable to hear the word "Fore!"

But the problem with hierarchies is that if you take it out on someone, they look to take it out on someone else. And when I was a youth, that meant the juniors. So if they saw a couple of juniors coming up the fairway they wouldn't wait till we were through before sticking on the greenside sprinklers.

We were invisible to the greenkeeping staff who would carry on all the maintenance functions they would normally pause for adults, as if we weren't there. I knew this to be true because if you got to play with somebody's dad, then all of a sudden they wouldn't take the flag out and start mowing the green when you approached.

Island Holes

A par-3 hole with an island green is supposedly Arnold Palmer's ideal "golf hole" because it forces golfers to be aggressive and go for the pin. Call me a dyed in the wool traditionalist but that's a load of old cobblers. Golf should be about making choices and seeing if the choice of shot you make pans out, not being forced into playing one type of shot. That's why coastal holes with a dog-leg across a bay give you a conventional land route and a dangerous cut-the-corner route. What Arnie was advocating is akin to golf communism – there is only one way. Blimey, that's almost an un-American activity.

It would be interesting to note if Arnie was being sponsored by a golf ball manufacturer at the time, because island holes are a sure-fire way to increase the turnover of ball sales in the pro's shop. Not to mention the resale of Lake Balls afterwards. Conspiracy theorists might be able to establish that the entire North American golfing industry is predicated on a certain percentage loss of balls via island greens.

In Idaho there is actually a floating island par-3 hole built on something like an old lumber raft which can be moored at different distances from the shore. You have to be taken out to it by boat when you eventually get your ball on the green. Island greens may be a bit crazy golf, but this takes the concept one step further.

Islands in the Stream

The idea of a floating island green raises all kinds of questions. For a start – what distance do they print on the score card: 120 yards to 185 yards (depending on how vicious the greenkeeper is feeling).

Does it bob when the lake gets rough? Is it possible to feel seasick on a "golf hole"?

If they anchor it with loose enough tethers do you have to allow for movement of the green when you aim your tee shot?

When I was studying for my degree in Kent, the rugby club had a celebrated annual dinner at a hotel in Rye. It's always been my experience with rugby players that the words "beer" and "enough" don't sit easily together; unless the word "not" is inserted somewhere between the two. Thus at around midnight when 30 or so well-oiled rugby-playing students were dispatched onto the streets of Rye, high jinx was afoot.

En route to their coach they thought it might be an inspired idea to go for a jaunt in one of the trawlers moored to the quayside. They had got onboard one and fired it up and were just working out how to get it into gear when the boys in blue turned up, and that was the end of that.

But imagine how much fun you could have if you hijacked a complete green. That is going to be a quantum leap above a traffic cone any day of the week.

Alternatively, if you wanted to combine a sailing holiday with a golfing holiday, just tow a green around behind your boat. It might make travelling through canal locks a bit hazardous, and at sea they're not going to speed you up any, but you'd be able to pick your own scenery. And no queueing to get on the tee either.

Handicap Bandits

People who consistently manipulate their handicap to their advantage in club competitions should be exposed for what they are. Bandidos. Forget the average over three rounds nonsense and the unified handicapping system as devised by CONGU or CONGA or Black Lace or whatever they're called, handicaps should be cut the minute you win some silverware. Simple as.

People Who Tell You: 'It's All In The Head'

People say, fatuously, that 95% of golf is in the head. To these people I'd say; "Try swinging a golf club on a links course in February in a Force 9 gale whipped in off the North Sea." I think that having feeling in your hands and fingers at that stage is 95% and what's going on your head is 5%, and that 5% is simply: 'Get me back in the ****ing clubhouse.'

Similarly, no matter how many hi-tec waterproofing 'innovations' golf shoe manufacturers come up with, on a miserably wet day with rain falling in stair rods, water will find a way in. Even if you have the new Duck's Foot-Pro, with new Anti-Aqueous MicofiberTM, tested to 100 feet.

Driving Up Your Backside

You're walking up the middle of the fairway and all of a sudden a ball whangs past your head at speed, launched by the pairing on the tee behind. Part of you thinks it was a genuine mistake and they misjudged the distance. Part of you thinks they did it deliberately in a bid to be let through or as an indication that you're playing too slowly for their liking. That part of you is about 90%.

In situations like this you turn and look to see some kind of acknowledgment that they've just made a mistake. A friendly wave, or a shout of "Sorry!". If they don't it's the golfing equivalent of slapping you over the cheek with a buckskin glove and demanding a duel. "My card, sir, we shall meet a dawn. Nominate your second."

In those instances a testy little stand-off can develop.

When I was playing at college in a staff versus students match, one of the students in the group behind battered one past us, much to the annoyance of the Bursar, a man of senior years with an impressively short fuse, who was playing in our foursome.

He responded by striding over to the ball and whacking it back towards the tee. This was in the middle of a competition! Being quite a senior figure in the college, neither of the lecturers in the group behind was prepared to query what he did. And to be fair, it was one of the best shots he played all afternoon.

That kind of behaviour without the *droit de seigneur* involved in our match might get you into a bit of a ruck on a golf course, but with balls flying further it's a bigger problem than ever.

Leaving Too Much Distance

Because it's easier to hit a ball mega-distances now, to be safe you have to leave a very generous margin of error on every hole. We've all played with big beefy uncoordinated players who can stride up to the tee and tonk it a brutish 250 yards on one hole and duff it for 50 on the next. And that's just the ladies. You can leave a massive gap between yourselves and the group in front, then look extremely foolhardy when you bodge it miserably only a quarter of the distance. Then on the next hole you think, 'sod it, who am I kidding? I'm not going to reach the players in front' and put one of them in hospital.

Allowing For Wind

Frequently on television you'll see professionals take a few blades of grass and toss them into the air, stare into the middle distance sagely and then hit an immaculate shot, seemingly unaffected by wind. When I do this, very much the same happens. The blades of grass fall to the ground, I stare sagely into the middle distance and hit a shot seemingly unaffected by wind. The only difference is that I've started it out right and it stays out right. At which point my partner says, "I wondered why you were aiming out there…" Despite many years playing the game I still have no idea what a wind from the side is going to do – whether I should allow for it a little, a lot or just ignore it altogether. Wind from the front I understand you just hit the ball low. Wind from behind is great, it's a free ride, but cross winds are a nightmare. On very windy days there are those that allow for wind on putts. To my mind that's one variable too many to account for. When you're putting you need to compute the following information.

a) Will I be able to get the club head straight at point of impact?

b) What is the pace of the green?

c) What is the slope of the green?

d) Are there any bits in the way?

e) Did I learn anything from watching my partner's putt

That's enough for me. If you've got to factor in the wind as well I might as well call in Carol Vorderman.

Americans And Golf

There is a tremendously entertaining book entitled *101 Sports Not to Play* by Adam Russ which takes a merciless look at the way America has adopted various sports and changed the rules to suit themselves. Rugby wasn't interesting enough so they invented a forward pass and called it 'football' even though kicking the ball is one of the smallest elements of the game.

They would no doubt have tried to change golf if they didn't come to it so late in the day. While the Scots and the English were building some of the most challenging links courses of the 19th century, the Americans were too busy dispossessing Native Americans and stealing bits of Mexico. The Royal and Ancient now has a firm grip on the rules of golf and long may they remain in charge.

American Golf Commentary

One the best adverts for (Sir) Peter Alliss and the whole of the BBC golf commentary team is being forced to listen to their American counterparts. Before the BBC start transmission from the Masters at Augusta you can tune in to the American television coverage on line. Awesome.

Almost all of their commentators are called Bob or Jim. Now I don't know about you, but the sentence, "That's a great golf shot, Bob" seems to have one completely unnecessary word in it. We're watching golf aren't we? Or do players have the option to make a rifle shot or a "soccer" shot?

Or, is the average American TV sports fan, sat at home with their six-pack of Bud and trans-fat rich burger, ever so slightly educated by that sentence?

There is none of the poetry and whimsy of Alliss or the wry humour of Sam Torrance and Mark James (himself a grumpy golfer of considerable note). Instead you get phrases on the lines of: "That's a strong effort from Choi."

It's easy to see why the nation is beloved of squeezy-cheese straight from the fridge when listening to American golf commentary.

Open And Shut Up!

Considering golf is such a precise game, where players have to be mindful not to rest their club in a hazard, not move their ball a nanometre, and sign for an accurate score, it's amazing how slack they are when it comes to referring to competitions. Americans refer to the Open

Championship played on a British links course for the famed Claret Jug as the British Open. It's not, it's the Open. And it's called that because it was the very first international tournament. The American Open is called that because it came after the Open and had to distinguish itself in some way. For that same reason we don't put UK on our stamps because we jolly well invented them, don't you know!

Contrast that naming rationale with baseball's World Series which is played out only between North American baseball teams. And a good job really because they can't even win the baseball gold medal at the Olympics. They've won it once, Cuba's won it three times and South Korea won it in Beijing. Arf.

Imitation Is The Sincerest Form Of Larceny

Eldrick Woods is a great name for a librarian but not a golfer. Apparently Earl Woods' son was a prodigy from the age of two, winning an under-10s competition at the age of three. So why not think of an original nickname instead of stealing 1952 British professional matchplay champion Alan 'Tiger' Poulton's.

Phil Mickelson

In the true latin meaning of the word, Phil Mickelson is sinister. I'm not being anti-leftist and he's probably the nicest guy in the whole wide world but there is just something about Phil Mickelson that makes me want to break out the custard pies. I don't know if it's the dopey "uh-huh" face or the lopey walk, or his embarrassing birdie celebrations or what. You suspect from the way he moves around the green that he is the world's worst dad dancer and that if he didn't have a team of sponsors behind him he'd be shopping at K-Mart with 'Rain Man'.

Blonde Ambition

And what is it about American professional golfers? Why is *The Stepford Wives* always their favourite movie…?

Compulsory Golf Exam For Yanks

Whilst browsing the Internet for references to the names of old golf clubs, such as the spoon and the cleek, I came across an American website which actually ran the line: "What the heck are these clubs anyway?" No shadow of a lie. Along with a follow-up: "So who cares, right?" This alone is justification for a compulsory examination for all American golfers to know their history before they set

132

foot on a UK course – a bit like the written part of the driving test. Or perhaps they could make it part of the disembarcation card; prospective golfers could fill it in whilst still on the plane.

Golf At The Olympics

One of my major irritations over the last 20-odd years has been the treatment golf has had at the hands of the Olympic Committee. At the time of writing they have proposed that golf should be re-introduced to the Olympic Games in Brazil for 2016. And not before time, I say. Golf is a sport that's got a universal appeal and is played around the world by men, women and children alike.

There is an impeccable observance of the rules, as we've seen with golf professionals like Stewart Cink who would sooner top themselves than think they got an unfair advantage.

I've yet to understand how a sport (if it is a sport) like synchronized swimming can make it in there when golf and rugby can't. Women with perma-tans, unfeasible smiles and 4cms of lycra covering their vital parts might have an attraction to a certain male audience, but it's not exactly sport. In fact, anything that needs music to accompany it cannot be called a sport. If they're going to have rules like: "any game that can be played in a pub cannot be a sport", let's introduce that one.

Similarly, small bore rifle shooting, despite its continual Olympic exposure, fails to ignite the sporting interest of our youth. To do that they'd have to set the targets outside take-aways in North London and get competitors to shoot from a BMW X3 driving by at 2am in the morning. Though having said that, America would almost certainly win that Gold medal. And Mexico would get Silver.

Even target shooting is a recognisable if crushingly dull sport compared to events they just create for the sake of the Olympics. If you've ever scanned your eyes down the list of sports at the Winter Olympics you'll see that they ran a bit short and needed to invent some. The one where you have to ski for about 20 kilometres cross-country with a rifle on your back and then shoot at a target springs to mind. Having enjoyed many an alpine holiday skiing with the children, the only people you see on cross-country skis are either wobbly and geriatric or bearded and nature loving. If the whole purpose of the sport is to to recreate the Norwegian resistance film, *The Heroes of Telemark*, let's be a bit more honest about it and have pop-up German stormtroopers appearing between the spruces.

ADVICE FOR FOREIGN GOLFERS

In a bid to foster international golfing relations, I have put together a guide to be given to foreign golfers when they arrive in this country. The British are often seen, unfairly I think, as reserved and aloof. Armed with this guide, golfers from overseas, especially France and Germany, should be able to break down those barriers, confound stereotypes and make many new friends on and off the golf course.

Parking Priority:

British hospitality, especially from clubs in the Home Counties, is legendary. They take great pride in welcoming visitors from overseas. When arriving at a traditional British golf club it is common practice for foreign visitors to use the car parking spaces nearest the clubhouse marked 'Captain', 'Secretary' and 'Ladies Captain'. In reality these people are rarely at the club. If a club member fails to notice the foreign registration and directs you elsewhere, simply point out; "I am from France," and leave it at that.

Playing Through:

Britain is well known for its love of history and traditional rules. Some of our laws often date back centuries. Following a rule brought in by Queen Victoria – who despised golf – women have no status on a golf course. If you come across a slow-playing women's pair, trio or foursome, play swiftly though them.

By all means give them a friendly wave, but don't feel you have to. In this modern era of women's liberation a few might try and resist what they see as a manifestation of the patriarchal phallocentric society. If women object to your playing through, there is a phrase that often soothes the situation. Try shouting: "Shouldn't you be at home cooking the tea, love?" This seldom fails to bring a smile to their lips.

Old People:

The same applies to people over the age of 65, playing in plus fours or tweed of any description.

Chipping Practice:

Even though many clubs now have extensive practice facilities, it is common practice for foreign visitors to be allowed to use the 18th hole for practising their short game. It is understood that you will be on a tight timetable, so pitch in there. Ignore any members who might point you to the official practice ground. Similarly, any club members who are trying to finish off their rounds on the 18th are obliged to wait till you have finished practicing. If they mistake you for a normal club member or perhaps an English visitor, diffuse the situation by saying something like, "Achtung, Tommy, for you ze 18th hole is over." Watch them crease up with laughter.

Royal Golf Clubs:

If the club you are visiting has the word "Royal" in its name – such as Royal Cinque Ports, Royal St. Georges or Royal Berkshire, it means that Prince Andrew has played there. These clubs have a special duty to entertain their foreign visitors royally in exchange for their Royal namecheck. Foreign visitors are allowed to play these courses free of charge. Simply turn up to the secretary's office to collect a scorecard and a complementary set of souvenir tees. Remember to bring your passport.

Club Professionals:

Most golf professionals in the UK enjoy playing an ambassadorial role for their country. What's more, they hate to spend all day loitering in the pro's shop where they are legally obliged to keep an eye on the horse racing results. They will welcome any opportunity to get out on the golf course with a foreign visitor. Therefore your first port of call should be the club professional. Fix him in the eye and say, "I'd like you to accompany me and show me the course."

If they do come and play a round with you, they will be highly embarrassed if you tip them or offer them any kind of monetary reward whatsoever. It is their joy to know that they are extending the bond of fraternity between golfing nations.

Eat Like A Prince:

Ignore all you have heard about the standards of British cuisine on your visit to this sceptred isle. We have more Michelin starred restaurants than Belgium, Albania and Angola combined. And nowhere is that myth more exploded than at a golf club. The stewards responsible for organising the catering for most of Britain's golf clubs are required to qualify as Cordon Bleu chefs. All golf clubs are personally inspected by Gordon Ramsay who sets demanding standards for using fresh produce and providing innovative menus. From February 2010 all golf clubs must provide meals on a brasserie basis, so hot food is available all day, every day and not just for 15 minutes between 1pm and 1.15pm.

Hoy! Shout The Right Warning!

A common mistake made by foreign visitors to British golf courses is the continued use of the word "Fore!" The universal warning shout to alert other golfers that a ball is travelling at speed towards them hasn't been used for over a decade in this country. Thanks to a popular television sitcom *Only Fools And Horses*, the shout has now been changed to, "Oi! Plonker!" So if you hit a shot towards another golfer remember to shout out, "Oi Plonker!" at the top of your voice.

If you are playing golf in Wales, the Welsh language equivalent is "Oi, dipstick, look you!"

Regional Variations – Wales

There are many fine golf courses in Wales, and some of the finest in the world are in Scotland. There are some subtle regional differences that foreign visitors should be aware of while playing golf in both countries. The Welsh are fiercely proud of their language. In Wales, no-one is allowed to speak English on a golf course, and so if you want to play at the renowned Celtic Manor or Royal Porthcawl, you will first need to obtain a phrasebook to make yourself understood in Welsh.

Regional Variations – Scotland

In Scotland, quite understandably, golf takes on a religious aspect. On Scottish courses, golfers must offer up the 'Prayer to Auld Reekie' before teeing off. This prayer is passed down from generation to generation and *nae sassenach kens* what it is. *Jimmy*.

Scots are a private race and take the evocation of their golfing prayer seriously. One can often see the Scottish golfer Colin Montgomerie muttering to himself. This is because he is reciting one of several traditional Scottish mid-round golfing prayers.

Golf has also inspired some classic Scottish literature. The great poet Rabbie Burns wrote his address to the golf ball:

The groaning trencher there ye fill,
Yon mashie to a distant hill,
The pin no' threatened o'er o'still.
His spindle shank, a guid whip-lash
Poor devil! see him ower his trash,
As feckless as a wither'd rash

Space prevents us from reprinting all 115 verses, but had it not been for his Auld Lang Syne and Address to the Haggis, then it would be foremost in his canon of works.

Playing On A Scottish Trump Course

Donald Trump now owns half of all golf courses in Scotland. Be prepared to comb your hair forward at an unlikely angle for teeing off on any of the Trump courses. Once beyond the first tee you are not obliged to keep it forward, indeed, the windy nature of so many links courses in Scotland will almost certainly prevent you from keeping it there. You are unlikely to be removed from a Scottish golf course for not maintaining a Trump hairstyle throughout your round, but obviously, once back in the clubhouse, be aware it might be called upon. Those with no hair or of too short a length are not obliged to buy Donald Trump wigs for the clubhouse. That, quite clearly, would be ridiculous.

Regional Variations – South West

Devon and Cornwall with their miles of coastline and mild climate are sometimes known as the English riviera. They have many fine golf courses that hug the contours of this fascinating landscape. At a course in either of these two counties there are two things to remember. Once you have paid your green fee it is expected that you will give the pro two Cornish pasties, one for him, one for the boy. So don't forget to visit a baker's shop on your way to the course. While you are handing them over it is a nice touch to say, "there you are my lover." This phrase is used universally in the South West as a form of greeting and does not imply any kind of intimate sexual relationship. Unless you wink at them.

SIMPLE MISTAKES

'Hmm, That Was A Long Drive...'

I have scored three points in a club Stableford competition by hitting an elegant 9-iron over a clump of birch trees from a contrary fairway before now. My drive had been a wildish kind of hook that disappeared off left, but it was okay, I had known that there was space out there and, it being summer, the ball had obviously run and run. It was only when I was teeing off on the following hole that I realised it wasn't my ball I'd hit, it was someone else's, yet there was no sign of any golfers on the hole.

Playing Off The Wrong Tee

Unless you develop Alzheimer's half way through a round this doesn't happen a lot on your home golf course. But on a strange course where they've just moved the tee boxes and there's no other supporting information, it can be done. One of the reasons it happens more than it should is because the sketchy maps you get on the back of a scorecard have all the cartographic integrity of Ptolemy's first go at North America.

For those who ski, the average French piste map is a lot better than the average golf course map. And that's saying something. French piste maps have a kind of freeform jazz accuracy to them. The piste is there or thereabouts and sometimes it's gone, solid gone. You begin to understand why they had so much difficulty defending the Maginot line in the Second World War if the bloke who drew the map had anything to do with their piste maps.

Cartographers like to protect their work by including a few small but deliberate mistakes, known as cartographers' errors, so that if someone copies the map wholesale, they can easily identify the reproduction. On golf courses you tend to get it the other way round, with 17 holes all the wrong shape and wrong direction with just one that's correct.

Map Fun

My brother paid in excess of £60 for golf + lunch at a well-known course in South Wales close to where he lives. He wasn't scoring, he was just trying out the course for a bit of rest and relaxation. As the round progressed he got increasingly irritated by the map of the place. The first three holes were fine, but the fourth wasn't anything like it should have been, neither was the 5th. His ire was stoked up by the fact that he'd paid a lot of money for his round and they gave him this crummy little map!

At the 6th hole he suddenly realised he was looking at a map of a golf course he'd played a month previously and he'd taken the wrong one out of his bag.

Wrong Green

Again this shouldn't happen on your home course unless Nurse has been very lax with the medicine. I'd love to know if there is any confusion brought about by those fantastically large double greens in Scotland.

Wrong Course

Occasionally people have turned up at locations where there are two courses and missed their teeing off time because they went to the East course instead of the West course. Durrrr – stupid.

I have the dubious honour of turning up at the wrong course that was 15 miles away from the one I should have been playing at. It was the Worcestershire Junior championship held in Droitwich over two rounds. We successfully got through the morning round, but over lunch the heavens opened and the course was flooded so the competition was abandoned. It was re-arranged for a month later and I duly turned up at the Droitwich course for my teeing off time only to find no-one else in the car park. My home club secretary had failed to tell me that it had been re-arranged to be played at Redditch instead…

My Roundus Horriblis

The simple mistake here was thinking that a sunny day would herald a perfect round of gold. My *roundus horriblis* was played on one of the most perfect June days. There was hardly a breath of wind on the championship course at Royal St. George's near Sandwich. Skylarks hovered overhead, the sun shone and it seemed like I was the only golfer out there. I could hardly believe it, a classic old championship course to myself on one of the day of days; what a break.

The par-4 first at Royal St. George's gives you no indication to the humps and hollows ahead. I scrambled a five. On the second I hit another drive down the centre of the fairway and foolishly thought my lack of practice for three months wasn't going to be a major factor. But could I find it? On a familiar course you know how far a certain shot will take you, and on a parkland course you have trees and bushes as reference points to note where your ball goes into the rough. On a links course you have the occasional bunker and scrubby bits of gorse and heather and that's your lot. What is worse is that there are all kinds of unkind bumps and hollows that send a perfectly straight shot sideways into the semi-rough. The minute it disappeared in there it became invisible and, with no playing partner to help it was impossible. I went backwards and forwards looking for it for ten minutes. I'd lost a ball with a perfectly good straight drive.

The round kind of degenerated after that. I didn't make one par. I arrived with seven balls, found another six en route and lost all of them by the time I got to the rough at the side of 17th fairway where I gave up and sulked my way back to the car.

Losing Clubhead Covers

What is it about clubhead covers that have a kind of deathwish to them? Look in any transport Lost Property office and you'll find a huge number of hats and umbrellas. The clubhead cover is the folding umbrella of the sporting world – they are made to be lost or go missing. They are the hub cap of the motoring world (as discussed in the frankly brilliant *Grumpy Driver's Handbook*). Their wish is to be free and run wild and spend time in bushes, in deep rough; lurk at the back of tees or adorn the side of greens. They hate the idea of conforming and being slapped onto woods and the odd fancy putter and sitting meekly in a bag. Though they're grateful for being moulded into even more far-fetched shapes than ever before and finally ridding themselves of that shameful stain that was the knitted bobble, they will never rest until they are fully liberated.

My attitude to clubhead covers is that:

a) "Woods" are now great big metal things, they're no longer made of wood and don't rust; they can look after themselves.

b) At least if they're left out in the rain they stand a chance of being cleaned.

c) I can't be arsed to fiddle about sticking a cover back on when I'm concentrating 100% on keeping the mental picture of where I saw my drive disappear to in the rough.

Losing Tees

One of the great mysteries of golf – along with the Stableford scoring system – is what happens to my tee peg after I've driven off. I would guess that I lose my tee on about every fifth hole of golf that I play. It's got so bad that I'm thinking of getting a tee-gun and loading a clip of tees in. Builders can get clips of nails for nail guns and it would work very much the same way. And how cool an accessory would that be – you could be like the 007 of golf, walking casually onto the tee and firing a tee into the…erm…tee.

Chris, who graciously subedited this book, volunteered the story that a tight-fisted friend of his father used to tie a length of narrow rope to his tees so he didn't lose them. That's my kind of golfer.

And that bit about the Stableford system. I do know how it works – unlike cricket's Duckworth and Lewis Method – it's just that I'm always amazed when people I see duffing round the course come back to the clubhouse with amazing points tallies.

One moment they're pinballing a TaylorMade Penta between birch trees like some indecisive woodpecker and the next moment they're in the clubhouse stepping forward with a look of false modesty to accept a small trophy.

A Masterly 108

My favourite simple mistake story, though, concerns a golfer who manged to score 108 on a single hole. Now, not even Sandy Lyle could score an 108 around the whole of Augusta's 18 holes, though he *has* tried.

American professional Dave Hill was playing at the Thunderbird Classic tournament in New Jersey in 1966. At one hole he scored a disastrous 10 which his playing partner had kindly marked down on his card as an 8. Hill wrote a 10 next to it, but failed to cross out the 8, signed the card and handed it in.

Thus when the official scores were announced he found he'd mised the cut by 111 strokes. His round of 80 had been transformed into an impressive round of 178, which surely must stand as a benchmark for failure in the professional game. The only good thing was that he would have missed the cut anyway, but instead of finishing second last, he finished plum last – by 97 shots.

HOW TO MAKE ENEMIES ON THE GOLF COURSE

This is a bit like saying how easy is it to push a stone off a log – or how easy is it to confuse a professional footballer with a childproof bottle top. As we've seen with my own list, it doesn't take much to irritate a kindly soul like myself on a golf course. Can you imagine how easy it would be to upset some kind of irritable pain in the arse? For those of you for whom the game of psychological warfare is just as interesting as striking the white ball, the golf course provides endless opportunities. As I reflected one time as I strode towards my next-door neighbour who had let out an unguarded chuckle when my ball hit the sign directing people to the 15th tee and shot out of bounds...

The Cough, The Dropped Club, The Velcro, The Bag Rattles

Making a noise at a key moment in an opponent's swing is the most unsubtle of actions. You may be able to get away with "accidentally" pulling the Velcro tab on the back of your golf glove once, but more than that and it's like grabbing his block and tackle from behind as he tries to make a key putt. (That would have a phenomenal psychological effect because he'd be waiting for it to happen again, but I think it's fair to warn you that it would be the last game you played at that club). It's far too overt. A grumpy golfer has his pride after all.

My brother, who has no shame, is always quick to offer to attend the pin and leans imperceptibly uphill, holding the flag parallel to him to reinforce the deception. It's become like his Eric Morecambe arm-through-the-curtain routine, his trademark move. Everyone he plays with has seen him do it and so now it's taken a kind of Vaudeville act. People expect it of him and complain if he stands straight.

Looking At Each Others' Balls

You are supposed to inspect each other's balls before you start off. This is so you can readily identify the ball of a playing partner when it is lobbed into the long grass.

When playing in a competitive fourball, if you're doing badly, insist on checking everybody's balls on the tee before each hole while adding chirpily, "Sorry, I keep on forgetting". The underlying message is that you think they're all cheating b******s.

Lost Balls

Golfers commonly look for a lost ball longer than the five minutes allowed. One way to endear yourself to a playing partner is the second his shot sails into the long grass is to start a small device that ticks loudly like an alarm clock or that board game 'Pass the Bomb' and set it to precisely five minutes. Once it has ticked noisily down to 5:00 it should ring an alarm bell and a pre-recorded chirpy American voice (like Buzz Lightyear) should exclaim – **"That's it buddy, your ball is L.O.S.T. Lost!"**

Practical Jokes: Last Minute Golf Ball Replacement

If you have a friend about to take part in a prestigious tournament, what better way to make him crack up laughing than at the last minute, before he is about to tee off in the big event, replace his balls. Here's how it works; while you call him over with a suitable distraction, another 'friend' nips to his bag and takes out his regular golf balls, his Nikes, his Titleists, and replaces them with balls sponsored by the Red Hot Dutch Sex Club, complete with graphic of topless woman brandishing a whip.

Thus when he goes to tee off and everyone announces what they are playing, he'll be "erm…using the Red Hot Dutch No.5". That's after he's emptied out the entire contents of his bag onto the grass by the first tee in a blind panic to try and find a ball that doesn't promote pornography.

Video it from a distance – he'll see the joke after about a year.

Mobile Phone Glued Into A Bag

Another great ruse that involves a bit more preparation than the last involves an old mobile phone. With the rapid advancement of features on most mobile phones, by the time you've got your latest model out of the box it's already out of date. Thus there are plenty of old cheap mobiles out there you can sacrifice for the sake of a bit of fun.

You'll need access to his clubs a day or two before his match, but experience has shown that golfing widows are never happier when collaborating on a golf course-based practical joke at their husband's expense.

You need a patch of vinyl, some PVA glue, and the old phone. Take all his clubs out of his bag and glue the phone inside the patch of vinyl on the inside of his bag. So basically if you looked into the bag, it looks like there is a bandage in there. Replace all his clubs and wait for the weekend.

As he is putting on the first green, ring the phone. But only for about three rings. He won't recognise the ring tone as his own and in that brief time no-one will be able to judge whose bag the noise is coming from. On the second tee, ring him again, just as he's addressing the ball.

After everyone has checked their bags for phones in the inevitable post-fluff enquiry, let the suspense build up for a couple of holes. The best time to ring it is always going to be when everyone's putting and nobody can work out where the noise is coming from.

Your (former) friend, of course, will not believe for a second that the phone noise is coming from his bag and deny that it is him causing the nuisance, right up to the time that it's discovered. Which it might not be. The more important the occasion, the funnier it will be.

Things To Say On The First Tee To Unsettle Your Opponent

• "I like those trousers you're wearing. They look *very* snug."

• "Look, could you remind me to take my medication when I get to the 6th green. I keep on forgetting and the terms of my parole state clearly that I have to."

• "It's such a relief to spend a day out of the hospital. Not sat at a bedside wondering if she's going to die any second...anyway, your honour, I believe..."

• "What are you doing afterwards?"

• "I'm glad you can't see the bruises. I really wanted that anger management course to be a success, but by the end, the guy was DOING MY HEAD IN! I'm playing a Nike No.5..."

• "You haven't heard what happened last time? Oh good."

• "I've got a couple of scones and a thermos in here and I thought we might have a bit of a picnic at that nice seat on the 12th. Do you favour a macaroon...?"

• "What do you do for a living?" Then five minutes later. "What's your line of work then?" Then ten minutes later. "So how do you get by?" Then fifteen minutes later. "I forgot to ask. What line of business are you in?" Then repeat.

PANTHEON OF THE GRUMPS

Every grumpy golfer has a grumpy golf hero, someone impressively moody we aspire to be. Just imagine the possibilities of pushing the grumpy boundaries if Russell Crowe played golf. The highest profile grumpy golfers are the professionals who are caught in the glare of the TV cameras and the Pantheon of the Grumps is where they should take their rightful place.

Colin Montgomerie

Colin Montgomerie is the archetypal grumpy golfer. He is a grumps' grump. Colin, a Scot, naturally has a lot of passionate Celtic fighting genes in his blood. So when some wise-arse yank shouts out from the gallery it's only natural that Monty should be upset, confined as he is to walking on down the fairway instead of selecting a No.3 Claymore from his bag, wading into the crowd and doing something ancestral. 'Justifiably cleaving a spectator in two' is one of those things that the PGA is trying to put a

157

stop to and in no time at all he'd be cited for conduct unbecoming of a professional golfer.

Colin is one of the most versatile grumpy golfers in that he can be grumpy from tee to green. Whether it's a spectator marching off before he's taken his shot or a photographer pressing the shutter too early, Colin can sort them out with a few will chosen words.

Actually Monty has the great gift of self-mocking and starred in his own grumpy golf advert for Kit-Kat where he grumbled at spectators for distracting him on the tee, on the fairway, and then, when Ian Woosnam was putting, snapped a Kit-Kat in half with all the noise of Concord reaching Mach2. Who says golfers don't have a sense of humour...

Nick Faldo

Faldo was a big fan of the greenside whine for those who upset his putting regime. Almost every long putt Nick missed in professional golf can be ascribed to a small movement of a spectator. You see from an early stage in his career Faldo incorporated Feng Shui into his game and when he settled for a putt he was acutely conscious of the chi energy flowing around him. He channelled this energy through the putting stroke, into the ball. The ball was guided, via the hands of the master, towards the hole. In Golf Shui the ball wants to become in harmony with the hole. The slightest disturbance will affect the flow of chi and disturb the putt. If he could, Nick would have asked all spectators to hold their breath at once. And some indefinitely.

When the chi energy was disturbed by an early camera click, or a cough or a beer can being opened, Nick would turn round and say, "Oh thank you very much." Sadly in the U.S. they have a total sarcasm and irony bypass and so he was just as likely to get a back: "You're welcome, have a nice day."

Boo Weekley

Boo is not a thinking man's golfer. In fact compared to Boo, Forrest Gump would be considered a dangerous, intellectual. Walter Hagen once said: "Give me a man with big feet, big hands and no brains and I'll make a golfer out of him" and you could argue that Boo is the apotheosis of this theory.

For those who read the chapter on Sundry Irritations and thought that my insistence on golf exams for Americans was little bit below the belt, try this one for size. When Boo came to the UK he was asked if he was going to visit St. Andrews...

"I didn't know it was the home of golf. I thought the home of golf was where I was from."

And what does he prefer – golf or hunting?

"I love to play the game. But my heart is really with huntin' and fishin'."

Does he enjoy the food in Britain?

"It's rough. It's been rough on that food. It's different eating here than it is at the house. Ain't got no sweet tea, and ain't got no fried chicken."

No further questions, m'lud.

Tom Watson

If Monty is the archetypal grumpy golfer, then Tom Watson is the opposite, the anti-matter of the grumpy golfer. If ever you wanted a gifted, considerate and delightful partner for a round of golf, it would be Tom Watson. Now it may be that secretly, when he gets off the golf course he's a complete bounder, donning a Terry Thomas moustache, wearing a cravat and chasing "pretty young things" in an open-topped sports car. It may be that he gets back to his hotel room after a round at Royal Lytham and pulls the legs off insects. But I doubt it. Tom Watson is cheerful in the face of adversity and if I could ever have had one sporting wish fulfilled it's not to score a hole in one with a bounce off the tractor shed, it's for Tom to have won the 2009 Open.

Thomas Bjorn

Thomas has an overabundance of Nordic, Viking rage-and-pillage genes. He's like a raging volcano ready to explode and disrupt European flights for weeks at a time. Thomas has got angry with Monty, angry with himself and angry at being left out of the Ryder Cup team. Ian Woosnam used his captain's choice to pick Lee Westwood instead of Bjorn, and the European team won 18.5 to 9.5, one of the biggest ever victories.

John Daly

Daly is the only man to have won two of golf's majors yet failed to get selected for the American Ryder Cup team. And his time is probably past, now. His grumpy behaviour has got him suspended from the U.S. tour five times, referred for counselling – alcohol-related or otherwise – seven times. He has been cited for conduct unbecoming of a golf professional 11 times.

Eleven is an interesting number because it was also the number of women linked to Tiger Woods at one stage. This list included many cocktail waitresses and two porn stars, yet Woods was rehabilitated into golf's mainstream a lot easier than Daly.

Trinny and Susannah or The Gok wouldn't even attempt to approach his selection of garish trousers. He's not a man who the French would say 'was comfortable in his own skin' and even that's radically shifting up or down dependent on whether he's got a gastric band fitted or not.

Mark James

The one over-riding image I have of Mark James playing golf in the 1970s is with a scowl on his face framed by that Viva Zapata moustache. I'm pretty sure he and Ken Brown got into trouble for misbehaving at a Ryder Cup dinner once, and look at Mark and Ken now, pillars of the BBC commentary team. Mark's biggest claim to grumpy fame, though, was when he left Nick Faldo out of the Ryder Cup team when he could have included him as one of the captain's picks. Faldo sent a letter of support to his golfers on the eve of the match at Brookline and James tossed it in the bin. I can only assume that like my wife, he gets outraged by the incorrect insertion of apostrophe's.

Jean Van de Velde

The likeable Frenchman (not a phrase you hear every day) is not a natural grump at all, but his 18th hole demonstration at Carnoustie in 1999 was one of those rare sporting moments when even the most shockingly bad grumpy golfer could have made better choices than Jean. He needed just a six on the last hole to win the tournament, a seven would put him in a playoff.

So what does he take off the tee? A 3-wood, or maybe an iron? No, his driver, which he hits way off to the right between the 17th and 18th fairways, mercifully finding a good lie. Given that there's a stream in front of the green and he's just pushed a shot, caution would say lay up short with a 7-iron, chip on and down in two for a nice safe five.

Non.

Jean takes out one of the most difficult clubs in the bag, a 2-iron and blasts it into an 18th green grandstand, the ball bouncing off into deep rough. Next when he could still go out of the rough sideways and chip on with the luxury of two putts – he decides to go for the pin. He hits his sand wedge shot into the burn for three. After contemplating a water shot and taking his shoes and socks off, *le* common sense kicks in. If he takes a drop out, he can still possibly get down in two more shots. He takes the drop and chips into a bunker. So, that's into the greenside bunker for five. He makes a decent recovery shot and holes the putt for a seven, putting him in a play-off with Paul Lawrie and Justin Leonard which he loses. Still, he won't be forgotten.

Tony Soprano

Should the head of New Jersey mafia family The Sopranos ever be brought to justice then he could probably plead "Golf" or maybe "Gwalf" as the reason he became a homicidal maniac. Just as nobody is prepared to take responsibility for anything these days – Tony could blame his frustration with the game he loved but never quite got to grips with for his multiple misdemeanours.

His silencing of Sal 'Big Pussy' Bonpensiero, his brutal killing of Ralphie Cifaretto, his careful snuffing out of Christopher Moltisanti and his desperate slaying of cousin Tony Blundetto can all be traced back to his failure to correct a regular draw on his 7- and 8-iron approach shots.

Tony was never that grumpy on the golf course, but if he'd been able to get in touch with his grumpy side, then there would have been no need for all those sessions with Dr. Melfi and the population of Jersey City would be a lot higher.

GRUMPY GOLF MAGAZINE

I've been down to the newsagents and had a look through some of the golfing magazines and I firmly believe that there's a gap in the market for a publication that embraces the miserable side of golf. I haven't yet decided on the title. It might be *Grumpy Golf Monthly*, *Grumpy Golf World* or *Today's Grumpy Golfer*. On the first issue I'm going to put a great big AMAZING FREE! GIFT (worth £20) headline with a bit of broken Sellotape across to show that whatever free gift was on the front has been stolen. That will be a great grumpy start. Here's the Contents list for the first issue.

ON TEST: The Top Ten Clubs To Throw
When you're in a rage, the last thing you want is a club that won't stand an impact with an oak tree.

NEW SERIES: Worst Tee Shots In The UK.
No.1 Scragdale Colliery Municipal Course
10th Hole: **"Gulag"**

GADGET OF THE MONTH: SatNav For Senior

Moments. Get round the course without looking bewildered and playing the 9th and 10th over and over again thinking 'hmm, this looks familiar'.

MY FAVOURITE BUNKER: Ivor Grump gets out his sand toys again!

INCREASE YOUR POWER GRUMBLES:
How to make players in front speed up
How to make players behind hang back.

REVEALED! Tiger Woods' favourite golf course hotels for a saucy weekend break.

ZONE YOUR GRUMPS:
Don't rush in and waste your whinges on the first four holes – learn to spread them through the round.

IN FOCUS:
Tajikistan – We try out three great courses, most of them with grass.

STATS CORNER:
Top 5 Causes Of Death On A Golf Course
1. Heart Attack
2. Lightning
3. Struck by golf ball/golf club
4. Buggy related accident
5. Partner homicide

FIVE MINUTES WITH: Ivor Grump
What ball do you play with?
Whichever comes out of the bag first.

What do you use to mark your ball?
A marker.

Do you have any little pre-round rituals?
Parking the car, then putting my golf shoes on.

Is there one particular shot you'd like to improve?
Anything that goes forwards.

What's your favourite club?
Wentworth

What's the best bit of golfing advice you've ever had?
In the West Indies I played on a Robert Trent-Jones course and they made me have a caddie. I hit three bad drives in a row and the caddie turned to me and said in a heavy Jamaican accent: "Sell the club."